The Architecture Exchange Workshop Series

3

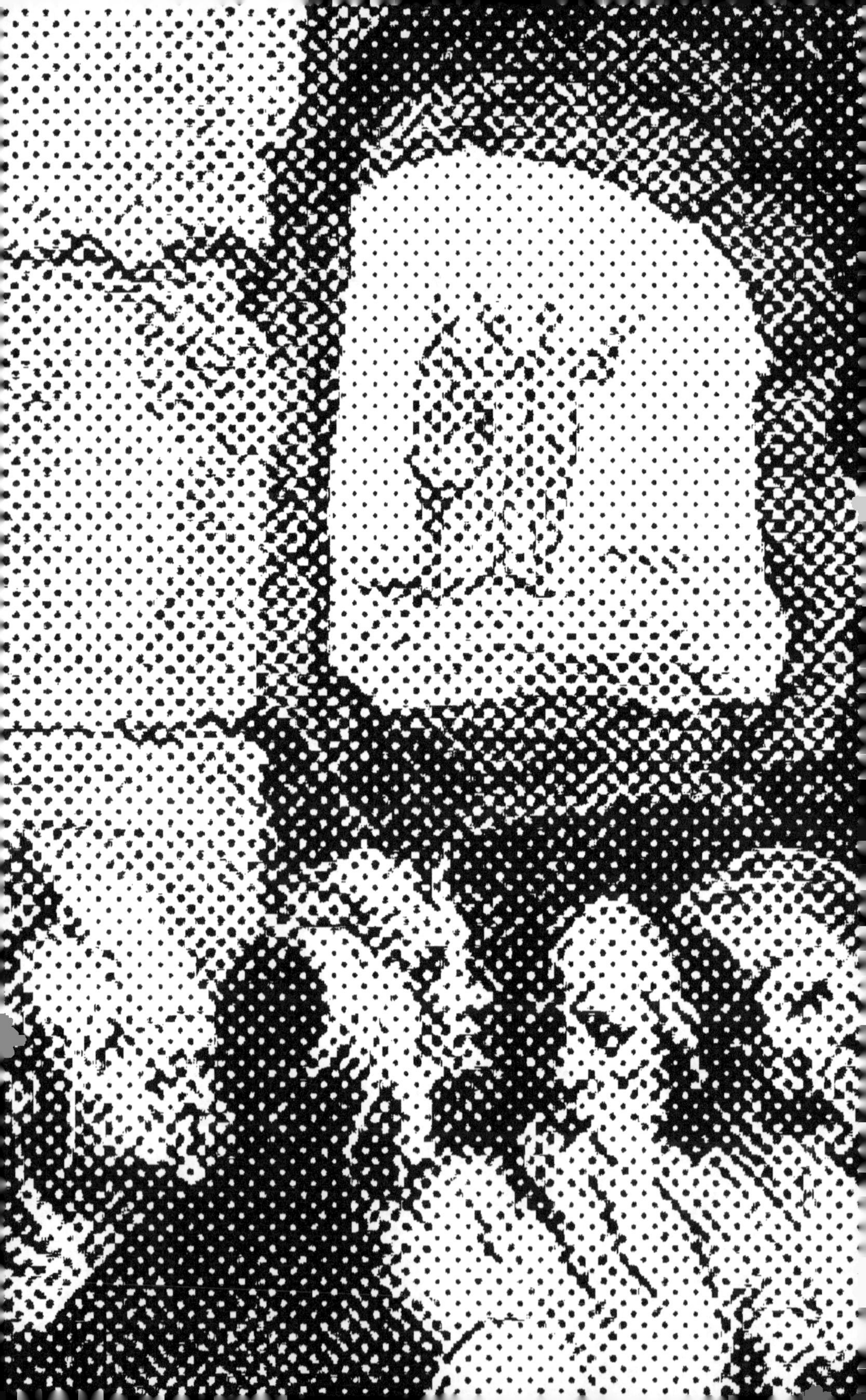

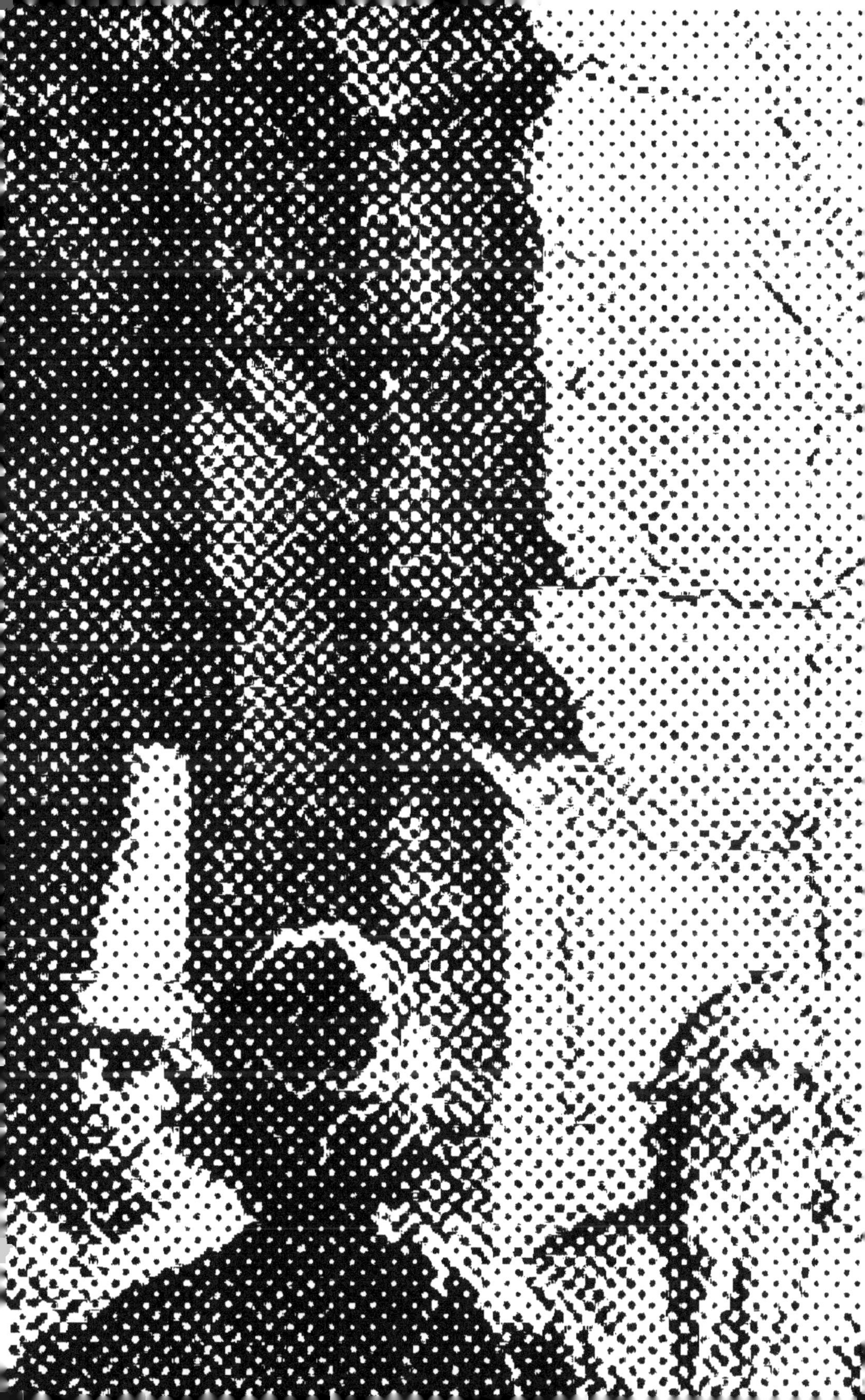

The Architecture Exchange Workshop Series

Theory's Curriculum

3

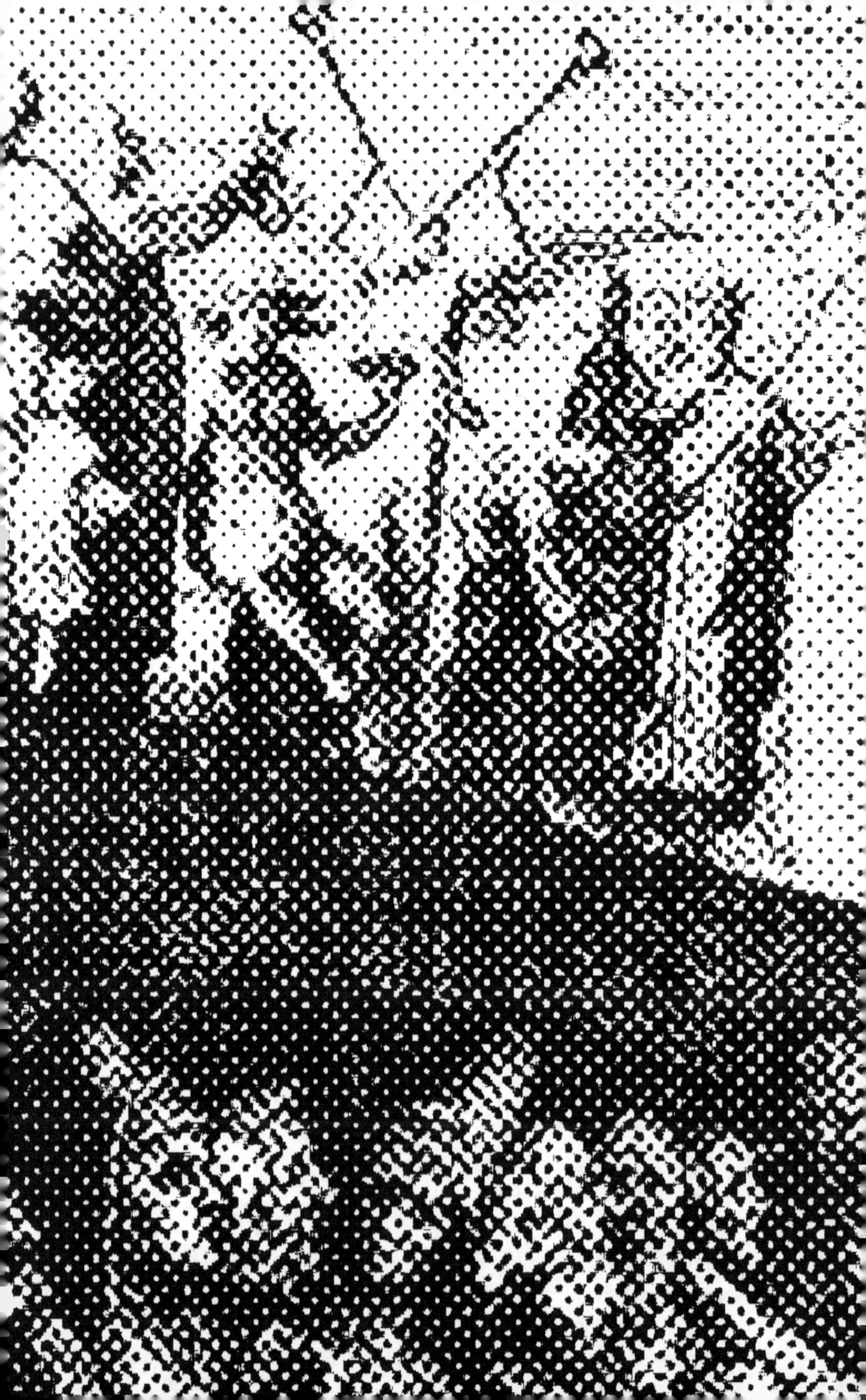

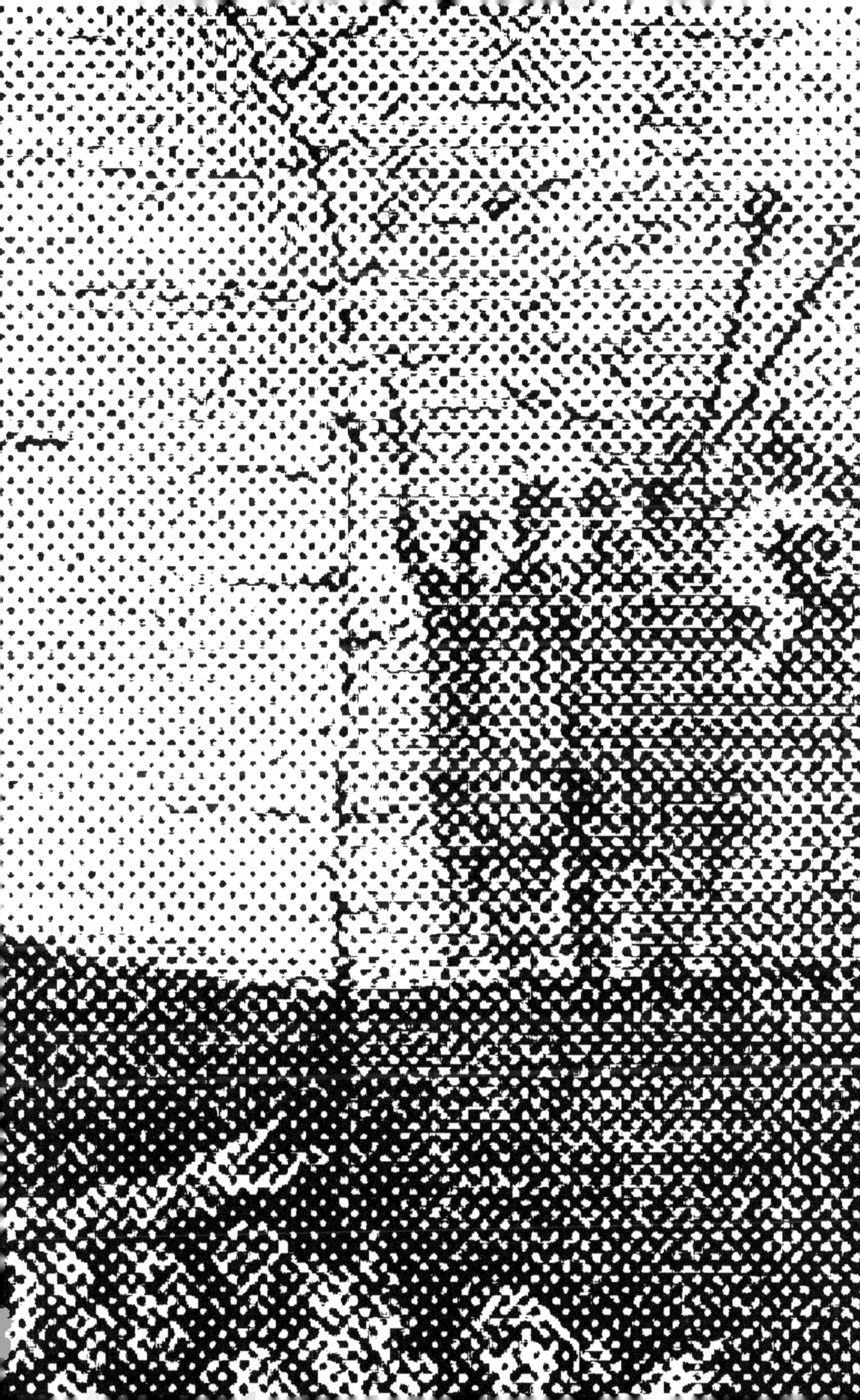

'SYMPTOMATOLOGY not only strains theory's capacity to project alternative futures, it also prevents it from saying anything about the present...'

Theory Beyond the Massage: A Thin Red Line
Jeremy Lecomte, 01

'It may be time to drop the term *theory* as a topic of architectural pedagogy and adopt instead a term – such as "architectural discourse" or even "architectural rhetoric."'

From the Boudoir to the Boxing Ring:
Or, How Architectural Theory Justified "Gym Crow"
Ginger Nolan, 13

'It may be the case that architectural theory in its most critically engaged orientation is somewhat incompatible with its sitting inside a school, inside a curriculum, inside a university.'

Schooling Theory
Joseph Bedford, 25

'Globalizing architectural theory can fundamentally challenge our conception of what theory is and what it should do.'

Is Architectural Theory Western?
Joseph Godlewski, 35

'theory is not a singular entity, nor a unified form of inquiry; rather, it is a process of interrogating, situating, and unsettling the present.'

Liquid. The Present of Architecture Theory
Ivonne Santoyo-Orozco, 49

'THEORY DOES NOT NEED YOUR PATRONAGE'

Theory Now
Jake Matatyaou, 59

'Gen Z is intellectually agile and forward-looking; rather than withdrawing into autonomy, they seek immediate material consequences for their actions.'

Generational Shifts, Criticality, and the Relevance of Architectural Theory Today
Gabriel Fuentes, 69

'Criticism's ability to challenge itself depends on greater participation... '

Against a Theory of Walls:
On Architectural Criticism and Decolonization
Elisa Dainese, 85

'Can we imagine aesthetic judgements to be shared but not universal?'

Globalizing, Expanding, Localizing, Situating: A Plan for an Architectural Theory Revival
Matthew Allen, 99

'... BINARY CAMPS ALLOW FOR THE STAGING OF DEBATES ...'

A Rough Sketch for a Model of Practice for a Hypothetical Discourse
Antonio Furgiuele, 117

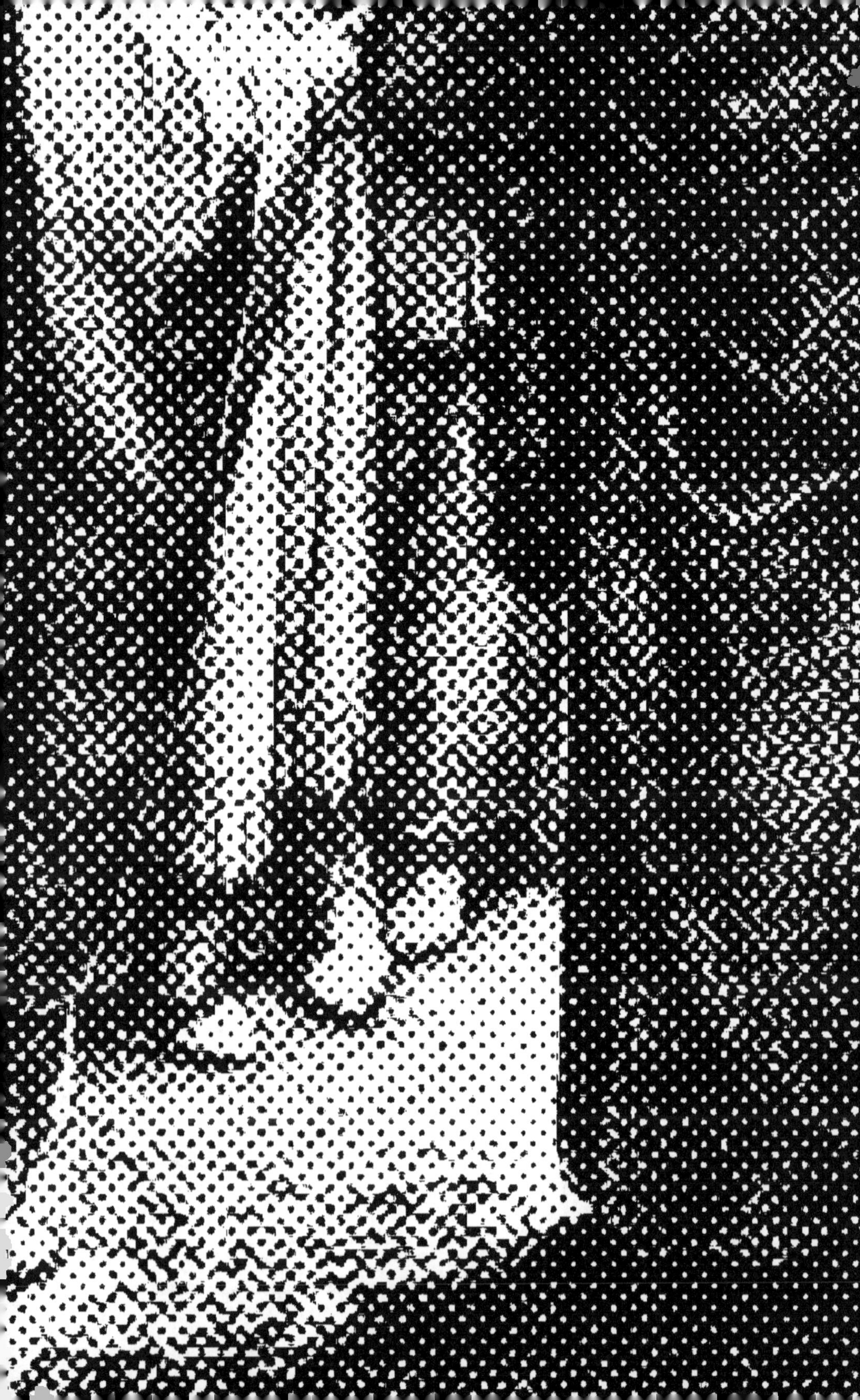

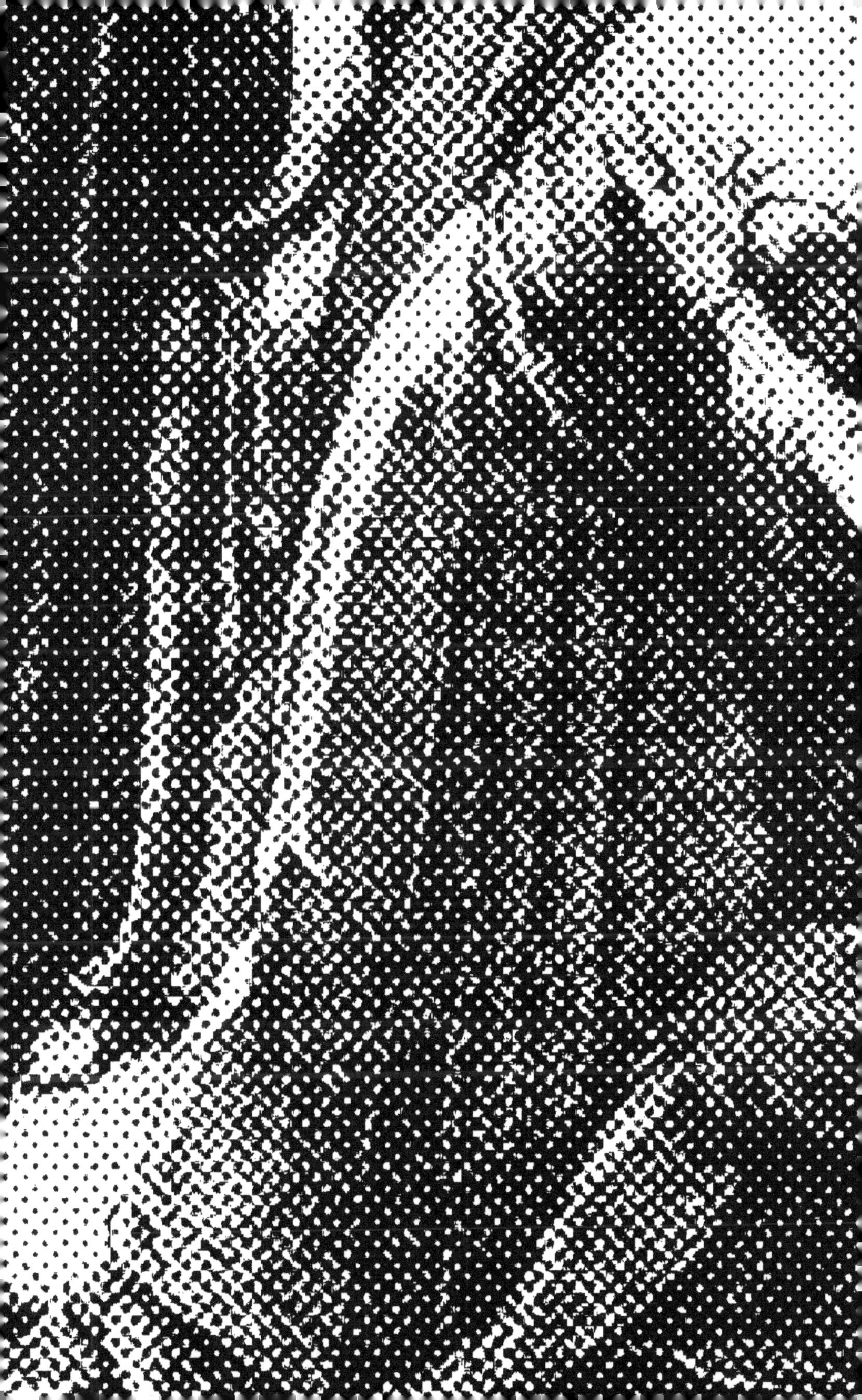

Introduction

After six months of lockdown following the outbreak of a global pandemic in March 2020, nothing seems so remote and yet so necessary as the project to which this publication belongs. The following book is the third in the Architecture Exchange Workshop series and like those which it comes before and after, it documents a particular kind of intellectual and social exchange; that which emerged from a five-day residential workshop to share ideas in person: not only in front of a lectern or across a table at a conference, but while having breakfast, preparing meals, dining, playing ping-pong, taking coffee breaks, walking, visiting sites, and drinking until late in the evening.

On this occasion, from May 20th to May 25th 2018, a group of twelve writers, educators, historians and—dare I say—theorists came together in residence to share their concerns and reflection on the fate and future of architectural theory, especially in regards to the reproduction of a culture of architectural theory within schools of architecture today. "The fate and future of theory" were the words in the original call used to prompt this collection of texts which each participant prepared for the workshop, presented, discussed during the five days, and re-wrote and edited for publication. They sound ominous but they reflect a much larger uncertainty at this moment around what we might call theoretical work within architectural culture today. The call for papers for a recent conference in Belgium on design and its relation to history and theory, for example, opens with the question: "are architects who write a dying race?"[1]

Of course, much of this anxiety about the fate of architectural theory as a discipline based on textual practices, echoes a now three decades old debate that has emanated from the institutional epicenters of

1 Cited in *The Practice of Architectural Research: Perspectives on Design and its Relation to History and Theory: International Symposium 8 - 9* (October 2020): 5.

Boston, New York, London, etc. Exemplary of the latest stage of that anxiety today is the voice of Michael Meredith. Of the 1990s, Meredith observes a contrast. "We read almost anything related to Critical Theory... whatever was published by Zone, Semiotext(e), or Verso. And we read journals: *ANY, Assemblage, October*. We read a lot;"[2] his point being that architects are not reading a lot any more.

Meredith's anxiety is felt by those who gathered at the workshop in May 2018, many of whom passed through those epicenters in their formative education. Yet it is important to provincialize this geography a little and place it in the much larger context out of which these epicenters emerged.

The purpose and function of architectural writing as a tool of critical, theoretical, and historical work was redefined in the last third of the twentieth century. Much politically committed intellectual work was undertaken in Europe during the 1960s. Think of the books of Manfredo Tafuri and Aldo Rossi in Italy, or the tracts penned by Reyner Banham, Charles Jencks, Joseph Rykwert, Robert Maxwell, Martin Pawley, and Dalibor Vesely in England.

Journals such as *Studio International, Lotus International, Architectural Design, Domus* and *Casabella, L'Architecture d'aujourd'hui,* as well as *Architecture and Urbanism* in Japan, constituted an internationally networked site of discourse in which "architects who wrote" grappled with the ideological and political legacy of modern architecture as well as the ongoing role of architecture in relation to culture, language, memory and meaning.

In the 1960s and 1970s, theoretical writing in architecture was thus in no way dependent upon the United States. Yet, by the 1980s, the well-endowed universities of the East Coast had incubated an especially heady branch of this international network of architectural writers; one that developed in parallel with the formation of "French Theory" in the same institutional topography. French Theory, as François Cusset argues, was the creation of the American Academy. It names a distinctly American translation of the French reception of German philosophy which went on to achieve a "global legacy"—from London, Paris and Ulm, to Moscow, Tokyo, Buenos Aires and Mexico City.[3]

---

2 Michael Meredith, "2,497 Words: Provincialism, Critical or Otherwise" *Log* 41 (Fall 2017): 169.

3 Francois Cusset, in *French Theory: How Foucault, Derrida, Deleuze, & Co. Transformed the Intellectual Life of the United States, trans Jeff Fort, Josephine Berganza, and Marlon Jones.* (Minneapolis: University of Minnesota Press, 2008). See also See Jason Demers, *The American Politics of French Theory: Derrida, Deleuze, Guattari and Foucault in Translation* (Toronto: Toronto University Press, 2019).

The rebirth of "architects who write" was sparked within this institutional topography by Robert Venturi's 1966 *Complexity and Contradiction,* a book itself attuned to the same groundswell of semiotic discourse that would lead to the flowering of French Theory. Venturi's book helped to inspire a generation of architects to write as much as build, including among them, especially, Peter Eisenman, who labored throughout the 1970s to foster what he hoped would be a new avant-garde in the United States based on a more conceptual, theoretical, and academic disposition.

Harry Francis Mallgrave in his *Introduction to Architectural Theory* has characterized this U.S. contribution to the understanding of architecture as a discipline, as constituting a "Gilded Age" of Architectural Theory; evoking through this phrase something of the decadence of New York's cultural contributions a century earlier.[4] This contribution was indeed a somewhat ebullient expansion of the practice of critical, theoretical and historical writing.

The image of architectural theory that emerged during this gilded age—largely as a result of Eisenman's institution-building—found its brief but lasting form in the Deconstructivist Architecture show mounted at the Museum of Modern Art in New York between June 23rd and August 30, 1988. The events of that year more broadly, not only instituted this image but made it from the outset a site of contestation. The shows curator, Mark Wigley, alongside his then roommate Jeff Kipnis—who played a similarly crucial role in the moment of the reception of Jacques Derrida's philosophy in architectural culture—both entered the field through Peter Eisenman's office and went on to play central roles in forming a new social grouping of architectural "theorists."

Architecture's literal "dans le boudoir" moment that brought this new theory generation together occurred in Jeff Kipnis's hotel room at the 76th ACSA conference in Miami between himself, Mark Wigley, Beatriz Colomina, Michael Hays, Catherine Ingraham, Mark Rakatansky, John Whiteman, and Jennifer Bloomer. What emerged was a grouping of a new generation of theorists with PhD's as well as an alliance between those interested in critical theory in the German tradition—including Adorno and Benjamin—and those interested in post-structuralism in the French tradition—including Derrida, Foucault, and

---

4 Harry Francis Mallgrave and David Goodman, "The Gilded Age of Theory," in *Introduction to Architectural Theory: 1968 to the Present,* (Malden, MA: Wiley-Blackwell, 2011), 123-158.

Lacan. Michael Hays had founded *Assemblage* in 1986, but soon, Ingraham, Colomina, and Wigley would join the *Assemblage* team, and Hays would signal his rapprochement between poststructuralism and critical theory in his 1988 editorial, offering an effective intellectual relaunching of the journals position.

As Mark Wigley often remarked, however, the full impact of French Theory arrived late to architecture; with its star rising in architecture just as it was dying in other disciplines and indeed, the MOMA Deconstructivist Architecture show was less a beginning than an end. No sooner had this particular image emerged than it was questioned by many observers. Mary Mcleod, for one, wrote an effective obituary of that high-theory image, which upon reading, caused Jeff Kipnis himself to sense its demise.

McLeod argued that in contrast to the Adornian conception of autonomous cultural production which she felt the new theorists espoused, they did not genuinely hope for the better society to which their strategies of negation were ostensibly directed. The new "theoretical architecture," she argued, made overblown claims that its formalist program could demystify ideology, and in the end the formal expression of subversiveness ultimately constituted a new form of commodity within consumer society, only to bolster the architects' authorial image.[5]

For Sylvia Lavin in "The Uses and Abuses of Theory" the following year, the only thing problematic about this image of theory was its faux avant-gardism. She listed the "abuses" of theory at that moment as being its use as an instrument of prestige; its use only to legitimate certain kinds of architectural design and inhibit others; its use as a jargon, pressuring architects to reference texts they barely understood; and a lack of rigor that led to interpretations of texts that made no sense.[6]

The contestations about theory that have been circulating in recent years, in short, have been going on for over three decades. They are a product of a particular characterization of theory in a particular institutional context at a particular time, and should not be mistaken for doubts about the idea of theory *per se*. They are linked to the convergence between the abuses of theoretical texts drawn from select parts of the oeuvres of Derrida, Lacan, Foucault, and later Deleuze, and

---

5 Mary Mcleod, "Architecture and Politics in the Reagan Era: From Postmodernism to Deconstructivism," *Assemblage*, No. 8 (Feb., 1989): 2-59.

6 Sylvia Lavin, "The Uses and Abuses of Theory," *Progressive Architecture* (Aug. 1990): 113.

neo-avant-garde formalist practices that soon became aligned with the emerging globalized culture of the "Bilbao effect" and "star architecture."

Yet embedded within this backlash against the deconstruction moment was a large unravelling of the alliance between theory and practice as well as theory and critique *throughout* the 1990s as architects looked to engage again in the new building boom that was emerging in Europe and around the world after the Fall of the Berlin Wall. As Rem Koolhaas put it in 1994, "Maybe some of our most interesting engagements are uncritical, emphatic engagements."[7] And as Stan Allen put it that same year, advancing the turn from critical theory to projective practice: "By and large, theoretical work has tended to fall on the side of critique and interrogation, what Michael [Hays] has termed strategies of resistance, whereas practice, for all its faults, tends necessarily to make some compromise with what Sanford [Kwinter] has rather elegantly called 'qualified surrender.'"[8]

A further advocate of "surrender" to what architects had been resisting for so long was Michael Speaks, whose career emerged from the very center where this avant-gardist and critical image of theory was being forged, *Architecture New York*, run out of Peter Eisenman's office in New York during the 1990s by Cynthia Davidson. Speaks had been a student of Frederic Jameson and had been hired by Peter Eisenman and Cynthia Davidson precisely to guide the project of "writing architecture." Yet he underwent something of a conversion in Holland in 1995 and began to attack the "American Avant-garde" for being obsessed by metaphysics and being limited by formalism: "the question would no longer be *'what is the essence of architecture?,'* (form, light, image, etc) but *'what can architecture do'* when it looks to its exterior, to the globalized metropolis?"[9] Such familial disputes among the younger generation of Eisenman's progeny in the United States during the 1990s—including Greg Lynn, Jeff Kipnis, Sarah Whiting and Bob Somol—lay at the core of what would later erupt as the "post-critical" debate in architecture at the turn of the millennium, though its origins

---

7 Rem Koolhaas, from Beth Kapusta, The Canadian Architect Magazine 39 (August 1994), 10. cited in George Baird, "Criticality and its Discontents," *Harvard Design Magazine* 21 (Fall 2004/Winter 2005).

8 Stan Allen, "Assembly 1," Mark Rakatansky, Mario Gandelsonas and Sanford Kwinter, *Assemblage*, No. 27 (Aug 1995): 39.

9 Michael Speaks, "It's out there... the formal limits of the American avant-garde," *Architectural Design* Profile, no.133 (1998).

stretch back some two decades earlier.[10]

This history still lingers within living memory in many of the institutions in which most of the contributors to this publication were educated or today work. As a result, it is the silent background to which their texts relate. The constellation of diagnoses, assessments, provocations and proposals gathered here, in one way or another, engage with the difficult work of assessing the institutional legacy of this zombified image of theory.

Yet, precisely because the history of architectural theory in recent years is not defined exclusively by this image and has a much more complex origin story, it needs to be addressed in more careful historical and geographical terms. It is a history and geography that scales from very large questions about the meaning of the events of May '68; to the contestations of Marxism throughout the 1970s and 1980s; to the effects of the new linguistic and semiotic tools on many university humanities departments; to the social space of East Coast Ivy League schools and the networks of patronage that thread through them—from Philip Johnson's high table at the Century Club to chains of pedagogical reproduction between teachers and students.

Each of the papers that follow attempt to assess this historical legacy at these many scales, but also from the vantage of the late 2010s in which critical attention has focused ever-more acutely on the effects of neoliberal modes of governance on the economy and the way that labor is configured; in which media-technical change—since the development of smart devices, the interactive web, the illicit scraping of behavioral data and the use of machine intelligence and algorithms to profile and target individuals—has formed into the sinister logic of "surveillance capitalism;"[11] and in which the consequences of globalization have

---

10 See George Baird, "Criticality and its Discontents," *Harvard Design Magazine* 21 (Fall 2004/Winter 2005); Michael Speaks, "After Theory," *Architectural Record* (June 2005): 72-75; Reinhold Martin, "Critical of What?: Toward a Utopian Realism," *Harvard Design Magazine* 22 (Spring/Summer 2005): 104-9; Speaks, Michael, "Intelligence After Theory," *Perspecta* 38, (2006): 101-106; John Macarthur and Naomi Stead, "The Judge is Not an Operator: Criticality, Historiography and Architectural Criticism," *OASE* 69 (2006): 116-138; Richard Anderson, "Tired of Meaning," *Log* (Winter/Spring 2006): 11-13; Robert Cowherd, "Notes on Post Criticality: Towards an Architecture of Reflexive Modernisation," *Footprint* 3, no.4, (December, 2008); Harry Francis Mallgrave, 'Pragmatism and Post-Criticality," *Introduction to Architectural Theory: 1968 to the Present*, (Malden, MA: Wiley-Blackwell, 2011): 177–93.

11 Shoshana Zuboff, *The Age of Surveillance Capitalism: The Fight for a Human Future at the New Frontier of* Power (New York: Public Affairs, 2017).

effected political transformations in many Western nations. Most acutely felt at present, from the perspective of writing after the wide-spread anti-racist protests during the summer of 2020 and in the run up to the next election to decide if the U.S. is to be governed by President Trump for another four years, is the heightened site of gender, race and sexuality in the larger culture wars.

Finally, the ongoing concern that each of the following texts address is not simply the history that has taken place *within* the institutions in which many of these writers have passed—Harvard, Columbia, Princeton, Sci-Arc—but the *history of the institutional form itself,* that of the university, as a home of theoretical work within architecture.

McKenzie Wark's recent ruminations in two books in particular, *General Intellect* and *Sensoria,* are insightful on the predicament of the university as a site of intellectual work today.[12] Wark is clear-eyed about dispelling the unhelpfully romantic images of grand public intellectuals—such as Sartre or De Beauvoir—or grand theoretical systems—such as Marxism or Freudianism—which purport to a total knowledge of reality. Wark is especially realist about the current state of the university within globalized late-capitalism. Where the ideal of intellectual freedom can be sustained only at the most prestigious institutions "propped up by the venerable seed money of slave owners, robber barons, or an imperial state," the majority of today's intellectual laborers would do better to consciously reflect on the conditions of their work.[13]

Freed from pretensions about academic life, Wark sees potential within the scattered field of knowledge production within the concept-forming work of a wide range of people—including film-makers, novelists, media theorists, and figures who often stray to the edge of their discipline—all working in a networked ecology made possible by the information revolution.

The chapters that follow build upon the kinds of ruminations about the fate and future of theory exemplified by Wark's recent books. They do not simply assess theory in its historical and future position within architectural culture but in particular the question of theory's curriculum: which is to say, both theory's place within the larger curriculum of a school, and the place of the world within the curriculum of theory.

The overarching background that guided the discussions over five days was a shared experience at the coalface of the contemporary

---

12 McKenzie Wark, *General Intellect: Twenty-One Thinkers for the Twenty-First Century* (New York: Verso, 2017) and McKenzie Wark, *Sensoria: Thinks for the 21st Century* (New York: Verso, 2020).

13 Ibid, 1.

classroom, located between the highly theoretical architectural discipline as it has been received and a new generation of students born after 9/11.

To put it bluntly, a history of theoretical concerns, or the tabulation of theoretical frameworks, or the roster of authors, which have become the standardized formulation for teaching architectural theory in schools of architecture since survey courses dedicated to canonizing theory first emerged in the late 1990s, have become outmoded by the march of history itself.

Wark's call to think about the relationship between intellectual work and the site of the university resonates with the ambition of the Architecture Exchange workshops and this series of publications. She recommends to our attention a number of projects already under way to foster an "under commons, with its own pedagogy and forms of collaboration"[14] and she models in her texts what it means to weave together the intellectual contributions of many intellectuals, foregrounding the dialogue between them. The Theory's Curriculum workshop represents one such form of collaboration based on such an emphasis on dialogue. Its mode of coming together was "in person" and physically and institutionally outside of the university and the constraints of quantification and performance that beset it. Its mode was also eminently that of dialogue of an especially literal and intimate kind, rather than a merely intertextual and discursive one; in which interlocutors dropped their guard, blurring the formalities of rational discourse with social life.

Theory's Curriculum thus represents a true dialogue between a new generation of younger thinkers in the field, that demonstrates, especially in a time of social distancing, the power of social proximity. It represents a reflection on the nature of theory in the architectural field and an effort to rethink the site and conditions for theoretical work within the realm of the classroom, its principal site of reproduction.

Joseph Bedford,
Virginia, 16 October 2020.

---

14 Ibid, 1.

Photos of the

Workshop

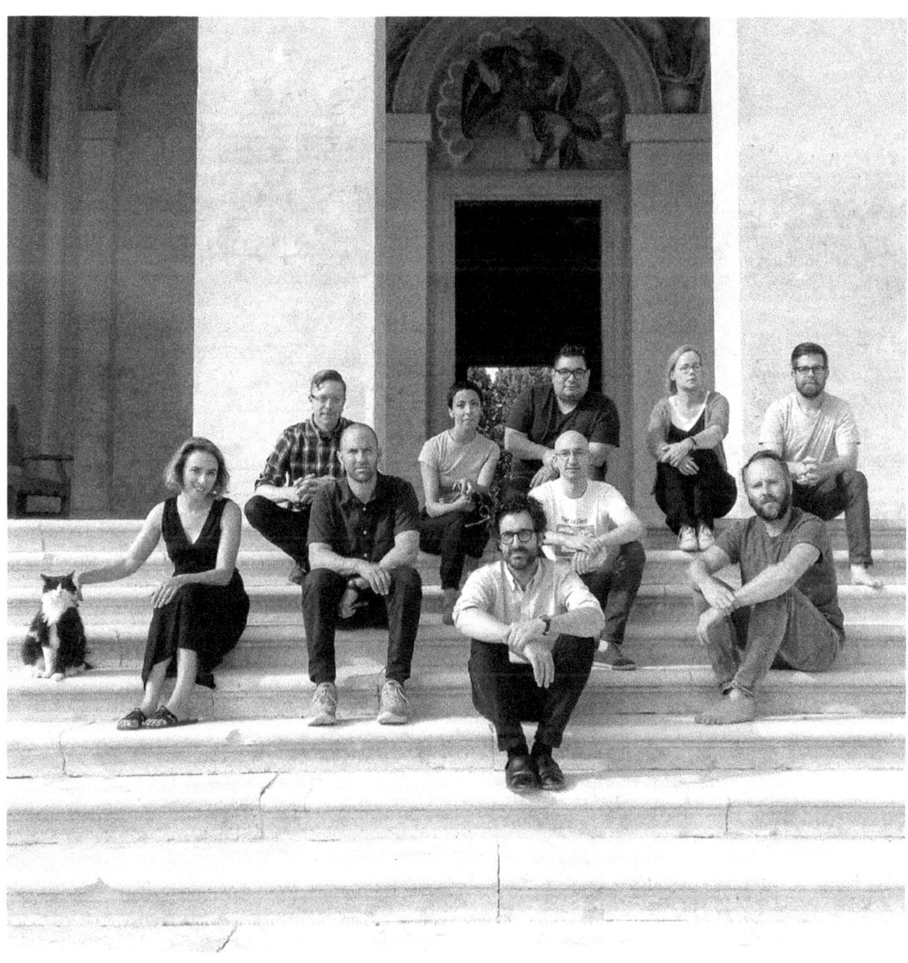

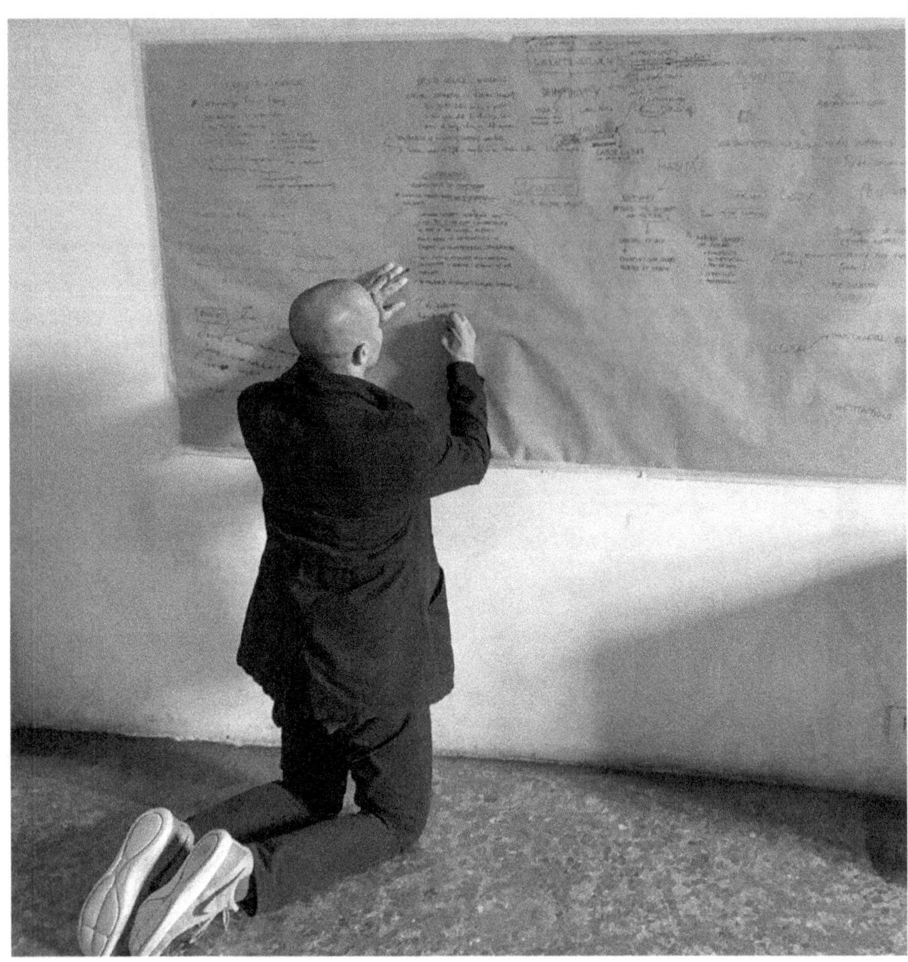

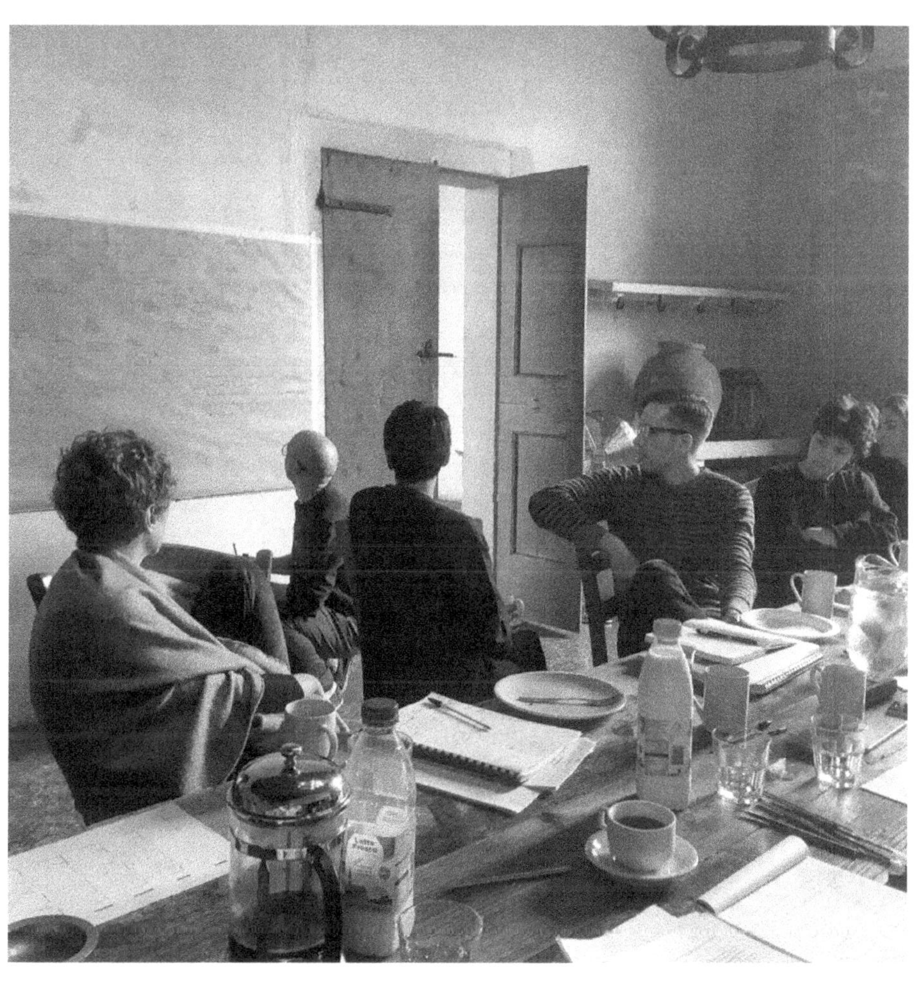

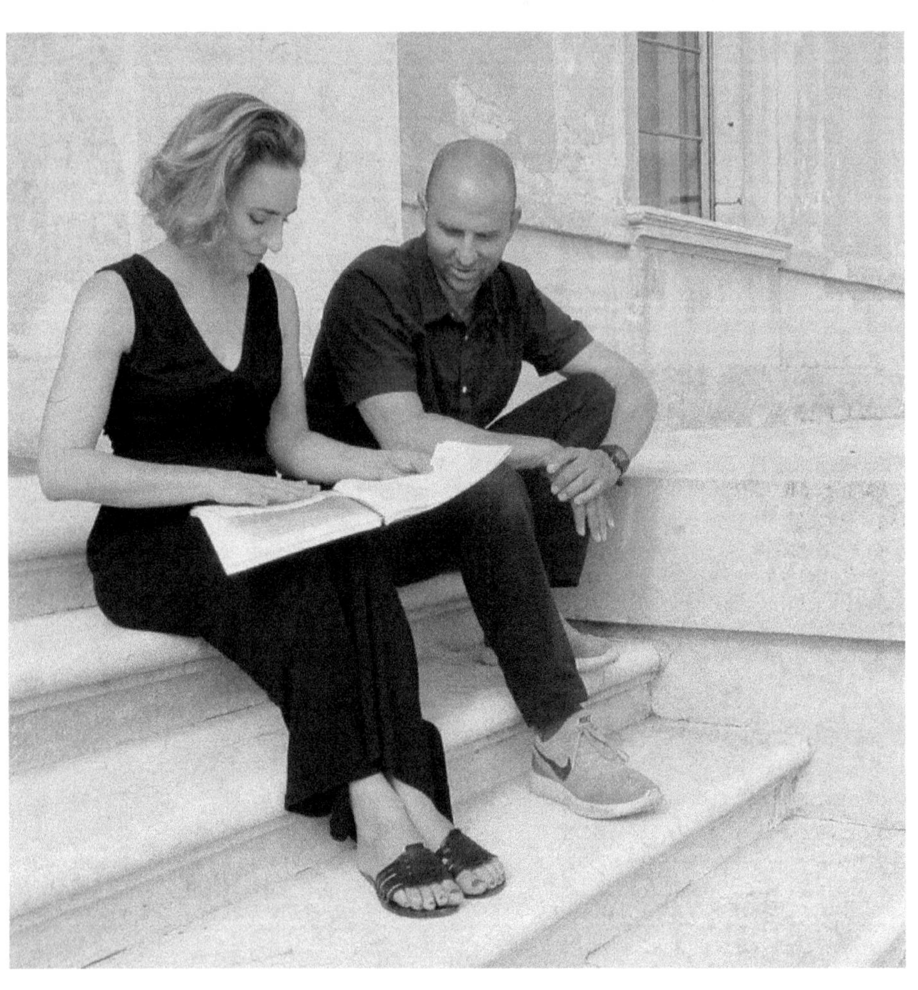

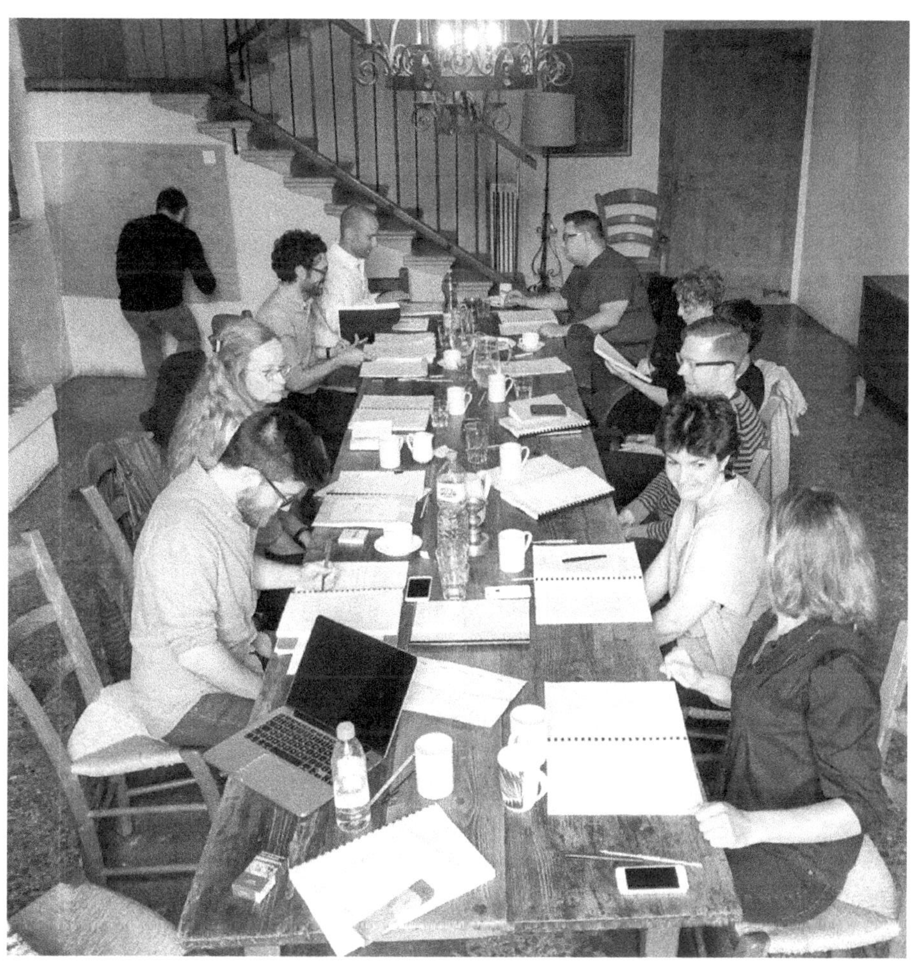

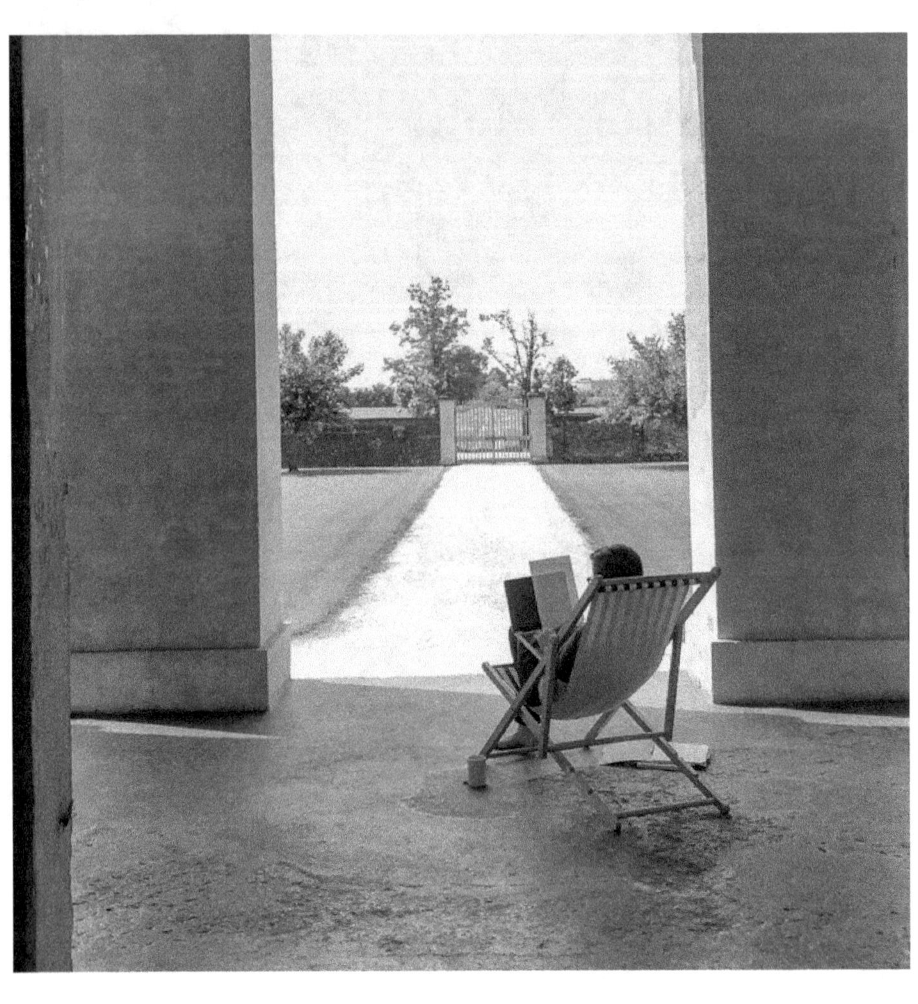

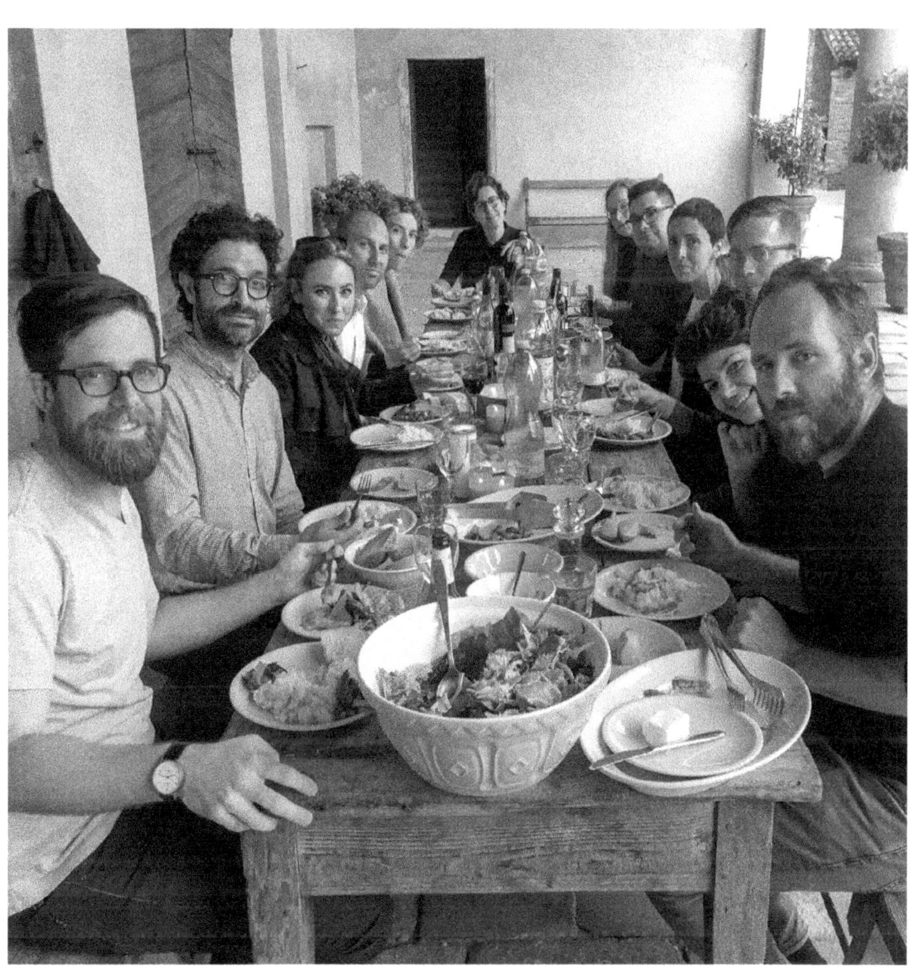

Theory Beyond the Massage: A Thin Red Line

1

Jeremy Lecomte

In 1967, renowned Canadian media theorist Marshall McLuhan published a strange book compiling observations on life and society as they were affected by what he called at the time "electronic technology."[1] *The Medium Is the Massage* conveyed a blunt message: everything is changing—"you, your family, your neighborhood, your education, your job, your government, your relation to 'the others.'" Why? Because "electric technology...is reshaping and restructuring patterns of social interdependence and every aspect of our personal

1 Marshall McLuhan, Quentin Fiore, and Jerome Agel, *The Medium Is the Massage: An Inventory of Effects* (Berkeley, CA: Gingko Press, 1967).

life... forcing us to reconsider and reevaluate practically every thought, every action, and every institution formerly taken for granted."[2] Illustrated by Quentin Fiore and produced by Jerome Agel, the book was a collective attempt to perform this argument within the older printed form. With a format that profoundly challenged the conventions of theoretical academic work—with images of strikingly different kinds mixed with text of changing sizes and fonts, words exploding the page, paragraphs upside-down, and multiple overlays—the book not only embodied transformations that, from television to early computers, were overwhelming the printed medium, but also anticipated an experience that has become all-too-familiar in the Internet age.

The Medium Is the Massage went beyond sheer performance, however. Behind the punchlines lay a clearly articulated argument: the print form belonged to the age of mechanical reproduction, structuring society by subdivision, classification, and inventory; by contrast, electronic media generated an increasingly immersive and globally interlinked environment in which discrete institutions would not hold sway. Making use of both academic sophistication and populist shortcuts, this book emphasized subjective interconnectivity, arguing that electronic media were fostering empathy that cancelled out the detachment and self-effacement inherited from the Renaissance. Instead, they were inaugurating inevitable conditions of collective immersion: a global village of simultaneous happenings.[3] Taking some critical distance from McLuhan's technological optimism, it is this society that Gilles Deleuze later (in 1990) identified as a society of control: a society whose global village dimension is also structured as a competitive market, a society that is the product of a decisive shift from a capitalism based on production to a capitalism based on overproduction, buying stocks, and selling services. In this society, governments and power structures control multitudes rather than shaping masses, and the whole system operates through continuous modulations rather than distinct enclosures.[4]

In their recent attempt to update McLuhan's book, Douglas

---

2 McLuhan, *Quent in Fiore,* and Jerome Agel, *the Medium Is the Massage,* (New York: Bantam Books, 1967), 8.

3 The different ways in which McLuhan described this new society are perhaps best summarized by this sentence: "The new electronic interdependence recreates the world in the image of a global village." McLuhan, The Medium Is the Massage, 67. See also 24, 26, 44–45, 52–53, 61, 63, and 69.

4 Gilles Deleuze, "Postscript on the Societies of Control" (1990), October 59 (1992): 3–7.

Coupland, Hans Ulrich Obrist, and Shumon Basar described yet another world, an extreme present defined by ever-accelerating production, communication, and consumption cycles—a society in which the newest thing is always immediately obsolete and where everything is shared before it has the chance to be experienced. Presented as a similarly performative "quick-fire paperback, harnessing the images, languages and perceptions of our unfurling digital lives,"[5] *The Age of Earthquakes* also appears much more formulaic and condescending than the original. Lacking the substantiated developments found in McLuhan's book, this mimetic enterprise profoundly misses the structural transformations behind the film Coupland et al. are ultimately dubbing. The book repeats on every page that the world we inhabit has become a world in which nothing can be firmly grasped, but totally overlooks how and why uncertainty had become such a central category.[6]

While *The Medium Is the Massage* may have traded some level of causal and critical analysis for effect, *The Age of Earthquakes* is a book that represents the increasing tendency of theory to become pure symptomatology. Unable to address the causes and look beyond the present it describes, such symptomatology not only strains theory's capacity to project alternative futures, it also prevents it from saying anything about the present that is not already given. The reasons why such a Potemkin village type of theoretical production has particularly contaminated architectural theory are certainly too numerous to be properly addressed here. But by looking at some of the structural changes that have affected French architecture schools in the past thirty years, and consequently addressing the material political conditions in which theory is produced, this short text aims to identify some of the causes and answer questions such as: Why is that some of us, as architects and researchers involved in architectural theory, feel that teaching theory in architecture schools faces such adversity at the moment? Why do we not always feel at ease when the word theory is

5 From the publisher's page for *The Age of Earthquakes*, https://www.penguinrandomhouse.com/books/317811/the-age-of-earthquakes-by-douglas-coupland-hans-ulrich-obrist-shumon-basar/

6 Following Ulrich Beck, Anna Longo has recently described this transition as one from a society of control to a society of risk. See Anna Longo, "Love in the Age of Algorithms," Glass Bead, Site 2, 2019, https://www.glass-bead.org/article/love-in-the-age-of-algorithms/?lang=enview; and Ulrich Beck, *Risk Society: Towards a New Modernity* (London: Sage, 1992).

pronounced? Why do we often feel that we may, at the very least, be talking at cross-purposes when this word is mentioned? Why do we feel that nobody seems to care much, and fear that theory courses could very well disappear from architectural curricula altogether?

The first reason is that while French public architecture schools were created in the 1960s and '70s by people who strongly believed in the power of ideas to transform the world (in close connection with sociologists, historians, and anthropologists that, at the time, strongly engaged with architectural practice and problems), they tend to be dominated today by people who have made their careers and secured their positions by systematically undermining this very idea. Happily mixing a diffused form of postmodern relativism with the opinion that serious politics should be nothing other than management, these architects and researchers belong to a generation whose members may disagree on many things but agree on the fact that theory is something that should not be taken too seriously. Traumatized by both the conservatism inherited from the old Beaux-Arts tradition and by the political engagement and ideological agitation of the generation that freed architecture schools from it, many of today's architectural educators tend to transform theory into an opportunistic currency, converting everything they touch into mere opinions and anecdotes.

The second reason is that this generation, now well-established in academia, is encountering students who have grown up in times of entrenched crisis and heightened complexity, and as a result are often ready to bargain their anxiety for whatever idea promises to be successful in the short-term. In this context, to argue that we should take theory seriously seems at best a luxury we cannot afford, and at worst an irresponsible move coming from a generation that did not experience firsthand the disasters engendered by the ideological battles that the postmodern professors claim to have undergone as students. Opportunistic opinions and informed anecdotes strike twice, as they appear both more relevant, more joyful, and more ready to use than any proper theoretical and historical argument. Complexity, we are repeatedly told, must be surfed rather than critically understood and navigated.[7]

The third reason lies in fact that higher education is increasingly

7 As Gilles Deleuze used to say in the 1990s about the developing society of control in which we live, "Everywhere surfing has already replaced the older sports." Gilles Deleuze, "Postscript on the Societies of Control" (1990), *October 59* (1992): 5.

modeled on the business school. In his recent critique of business schools, Martin Parker (a management professor who has taught in various British business schools since 1995) deplores how theory, in this context, has increasingly become a keyword for ideological ready-mades: "Because it borrows the gown and mortarboard of the university, and cloaks its knowledge in the apparatus of science—journals, professors, big words—it is relatively easy to imagine that the knowledge the business school sells and the way that it sells it [is] somehow less vulgar and stupid than it really is."[8] Ironically, much of what business schools like to borrow from the university is precisely what universities tend to trade for the supposedly more pragmatic, practical and efficient mechanisms found in business schools. Considering the complex relationship architects entertain with philosophy and theory, it is probably not surprising that they too are looking more eagerly to business schools over universities (especially university humanities departments). What Parker bluntly describes of the way business schools sell knowledge may increasingly apply to architecture schools: because they borrow the gown and mortarboard of the university, and cloak their knowledge in the apparatus of science—research by projects, PhDs, big claims—it is relatively easy to imagine that the knowledge that architecture schools produce and the way they valorize it is somehow less vulgar and superficial than it often is.

The fourth reason is probably both the most determinant and the hardest to grasp. Looking at the shared impetus to develop partnerships and joint curricula between architecture schools and business schools, one is forced to conclude that the difficult position that theory occupies in architecture schools may only reflect the increasingly marginal position it occupies in society. In a society almost entirely governed by capitalist competition, business schools do not occupy the best building on campus only because they can attract and generate more money, but also because they are increasingly seen as the most legitimate educational institutions. In fact, what the Bologna Process has incrementally instituted in the European higher education system since 1999 is nothing other than the idea (already long established in the

8 Martin Parker, "Why we should bulldoze the business school," *The Guardian,* April 27, 2018,https://www.theguardian.com/news/2018/apr/27/bulldoze-the-business-school. For a thorough presentation of his arguments, see Martin Parker, *Shut Down the Business School: What Is Wrong With Management Education* (London: Pluto Press, 2018). Parker, a professor in the School of Management at the University of Bristol, has taught in business schools for more than twenty years.

United States) that academic degrees should be treated as currency in a supposedly free and open economic market.[9] This coordinated expansion of the business ethos throughout higher education has also profoundly transformed the role attributed to theory. For those who entertain the illusion that using the same words means we are talking about the same things (e.g. Aren't businessmen and architects equally working on projects? Aren't philosophy and marketing equally interested in concepts?), theory gradually appeared to provide nothing other than convenient mechanisms of evaluation. Reduced to measuring standards, theory became a commodity amongst others: what counts is not what we talk about, but the fact that we use the same words and refer to the same quotes.

The fifth reason why theory is at once misrepresented and marginalized in architecture curricula necessitates some generational introspection. The diagnosis I have offered about the students we encounter in the schools where we teach can apply equally to us. Occupying increasingly precarious positions in an increasingly competitive environment in which our colleagues and friends are often our rivals, facing students to whom we may appear as Stakhanovites without a cause,[10] we often struggle more than we actually work. The main difference is that, while our students tend to look for pragmatic solutions to their existential anxiety, we tend to counter the depression this situation creates either by taking refuge in the romantic memory of the role that theory played in the emancipatory movements of the '60s and '70s, or seeking peace in a vain ideal of erudition we cannot really afford.

The truth is that the global political situation we face has nothing to do with the historical moment we continue to revere as a golden era (i.e. the sequence in which architectural theory's heyday corresponded to a strong equivalence, in the '60s and '70s, between social and political emancipatory movements and the critical theory we have been trained in).[11] The historical demise of that moment has impacted our generation

---

9 For a brilliantly synthetic portrait of the way that capitalist modes of evaluation pervade society at large (with a notable focus on work, education, and popular culture), see Mark Fisher, *Capitalist Realism: Is There No Alternative?* (Winchester: Zero Books, 2010).

10 In Soviet Russia, this term referred to the workers who, modeling themselves after Alexey Stakhanov (a particularly productive miner whom Soviet propaganda made a hero in 1935), were considered to be exceptionally hard—working, zealous citizens dedicated to the communist cause.

11 See notably Terry Eagleton, *After Theory* (London: Basic Books, 2003).

even more, since we have been trained by and through reading its main protagonists. From German ideological critique to French post-structuralism, most of the references of postwar architectural theory were generated in relation to material political conditions that have since largely disappeared. It is probably time to recognize that critical theory as we know it (and have been taught it) may depend upon a disciplinary social model that has receded into the background. More complex, more diffused, and more insidious, the dynamics of control described by Deleuze have also generated an intellectual discourse grounded in the idea that theory was never anything but disguised ideology, that the only true form of knowledge is found through empirical research, and that the task of any real intellectual is less to theorize than to guard against any theoretical bias.

One may say that, fortunately enough, any proper introduction to philosophical and theoretical texts reveals the trick that this move veils: insisting that anything other than empiricism is fraught with ideology attempts to situate empiricism itself beyond rational inquiry, revealing the truly ideological nature of the condemnation. But who can still afford the time and dedication to properly read and engage with these texts? Like convinced neoliberals who accuse anyone who dares to question their natural truths (i.e. the fact that humans are driven by self-interested choices, or that the market is the only valid form of social organization) of being dangerous ideologues, ideology-free empiricists tend to expose their dogmatic belief in phenomenological immediacy. While the first group cannot escape showing themselves to be gamblers disguised as political economists, the second group cannot appear as anything other than theologians disguised as serious scientists. Yet, in the present context, gamblers and theologians may find more supporters than serious political economists and scientists.

Far from simply presenting us with new questions to explore, the generalized uncertainty that characterizes a society in which everything is assessed today by risk calculation has also transformed the conditions from which we can address them.[12] In *The Medium Is the Massage,* McLuhan navigates the same territory as the architectural theory of his time. Between syntax on one hand and context on the other, and architectural form as an autonomous language on one hand versus the relation between architecture and the city on the other, the architectural debate of the so-called golden era was structured by polarities solidly entrenched in the social, material, and technological transformations

---

12 Longo, "Love in the Age of Algorithms."

that affected society at large. Today, increasingly undermined by the five dynamics I have listed above, theory has become a form of symptomatology that, condemned to mimicry, fails to construct such polarities. From climate change to the computational revolution, and from the deepening of economic inequalities to the development of social, gendered, and racial hierarchies, the issues we are confronted by today demand more than the form of neutral architectural symptomatology they are generally met with.

To translate these issues into proper architectural questions, we must start by recognizing that the golden age we often refer to when it comes to both architectural and critical theory may be less a model than a historical anomaly. Without giving way to nostalgia, we must postulate, assess, and practice robust and committed theoretical work to identify and name the causes behind the symptoms. Even from a position of minority, this work needs to mobilize the forces of intelligence against all forms of commodified arrogance, in order to constantly destabilize established discourses and powers, and to continue to insist that other worlds are possible. As Michel Foucault has argued and persistently put into practice, the critique of the present must never be understood in purely reactive terms, but rather as "an attitude, an ethos, a philosophical life in which the critique of what we are is at one and the same time the historical analysis of the limits that are imposed on us and an experiment with the possibility of going beyond them."[13] Understood in this way, theory is inseparable from both historical analysis and speculative thought. Against those who may be too prone to dive into purely imaginary worlds, we must assess the lessons of historical facts. Against those who may indulge in serial factuality, we must claim that there is no intellectual orientation without the revisable mechanics of theoretical speculation. In other words, theory is ultimately that through which one can cultivate both a capacity to describe why things are the way they are, and to imagine that they could be radically different. Because, as Quentin Meillassoux has beautifully shown, theory

13 Michel Foucault, "What is Enlightenment?", in The Foucault Reader, ed. Paul Rabinow (New York: Pantheon Books, 1984), 49. See also the introductory lectures to both his 1977-78 and 1982-83 lectures at the Collège de France: Michel Foucault, *Security, Territory, Population: Lectures at the Collège De France, 1977-78,* eds. François Ewald and Michel Senellart, trans. Alessandro Fontana (New York: Palgrave Macmillan, 2007) and Michel Foucault, *The Government of Self and Others: Lectures at the Collège De France, 1982-83,* eds. François Ewald and Michel Senellart, trans. Graham Burchell (New York: Palgrave Macmillan, 2011).

ultimately reveals that everything is contingent, such a philosophical conception of theory is the better antidote to an established order of things that an increasing number of people would like everyone to simply accept as self-evident.[14]

In 1967, McLuhan talked about a "shock of recognition."[15] Acknowledging that the social promiscuity engendered by electronic media compelled commitment to and participation in dynamics affecting everyone, he stated the necessity of transforming our educational institutions:

> It is a matter of the greatest urgency that our educational institutions realize that we now have civil war among these environments created by media other than the printed word. The classroom is now in a vital struggle for survival with the immensely persuasive "outside" world created by new informational media. Education must shift from instruction, from imposing of stencils, to discovery—to probing and exploration and to the recognition of the language of forms.[16]

Today, the vital struggle concerns the way exploration itself is increasingly subjected to economically grounded and algorithmically mediated forms of risk calculation. In a society in which the main goal in anything is to decide how much to invest today in order to sell at the best price tomorrow, theory has become all the more fragile. Contrary to what books such as *The Age of Earthquakes* endorse and perform, educational institutions must realize that theory cannot be restricted to *expressing* uncertainty. If theory is not about neutral, established knowledge, it is also not about better mastering the manufactured risks we are increasingly compelled to navigate. In this context, what we must expect from theory is neither the simple diversification of inputs (i.e. the relaying of an array of points of view) nor the provision of overarching concerns and principles (i.e. the classical image of the distant scholar possessing universal truth), but that it enhance our capacity for the construction of other possible worlds.

This is not entirely new. If theory is crucial to architecture, it is

14 See Quentin Meillassoux, *After Finitude. An Essay on the Necessity of Contingency*, trans. Ray Brassier (London: Continuum, 2008).

15 McLuhan, *The Medium Is the Massage*, 24.

16 McLuhan, *The Medium Is the Massage*, 100.

because of the central role it historically played in the development of a discipline that can look forward rather than merely applying a given canon and, by being reflexive in its quest for autonomy, can question its practice and its role in society. Since the Renaissance, architectural theory has been most necessary when it has allowed architecture to be self-reflective and, as such, both critical and innovative. Rather than saving the world or designing the revolution that we need, the task we ascribe first to theory in relation to architecture should be to relentlessly question the role its practice plays in society, forcing it to constantly revise both its aims and its means.

It is possible that, in the context of the present computational revolution, such a task may necessitate disconnecting theory from the alphabetical and print technologies to which it has historically been bound (notably by engaging more deeply with coding and computational modeling), but as with most technological shifts, there is much to lose here by thinking in terms of pure substitution. In any case, theory no longer naively asks us to look forward, it also stresses the necessity of articulating speculations about what the future of teaching theory could and should be to the lucid and uncompromising analysis of the conditions we are facing in the present. The problems we are confronted by today (first and foremost global warming and the related ecological collapse) raise questions before which no one can claim neutrality without implicitly endorsing the established idea that there is no alternative.[17] In times when we are reminded constantly of the imminent catastrophe (be it economic, social, ecological, or anthropological), to avoid questioning the symptom is to be complicit in its cause. Theory, from this point of view, must be cultivated as a tool to cut through the information overload, to show that there is something beyond risk and probabilities. Theory is about deepening the shocks of recognition, but theory must look beyond the symptoms. Theory is not neutral. Theory is not the massage. •

---

17 This is not just an old trope but has many current proponents, as two recent examples illustrate: Valerio Olgiati and Markus Breitschmidt, *Non-Referential Architecture* (Basel: Simonett & Baer, 2018); and the editorial of the latest issue of San Rocco (2018) entitled "1966." The way in which Olgiati and Breitschmidt explicitly frame their "analytical-theoretical attempts" as a collection of "self-evident arguments" is a case in point to understand the combined arrogance, authority, and stupidity that characterize such positions.

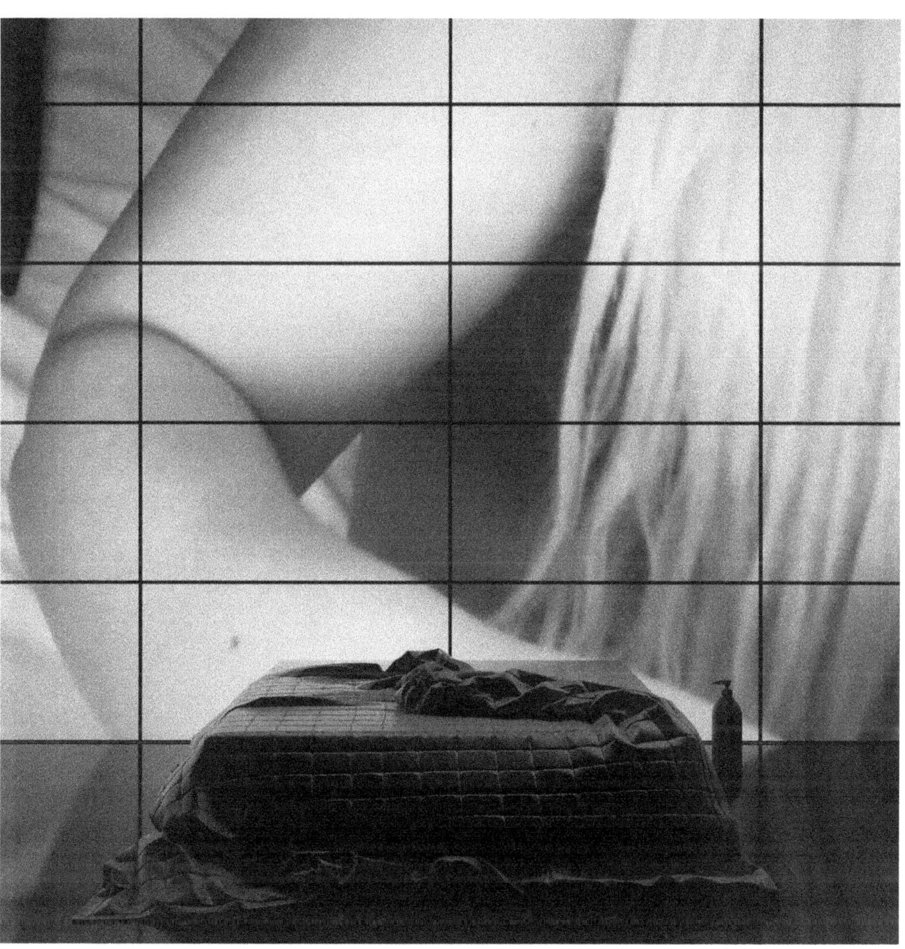

Image credit: UHO, 2020

From the Boudoir to the Boxing Ring: Or, How Architectural Theory Justified "Gym Crow"

Ginger Nolan

THEORY IN THE BOXING RING

It may be time to drop the term *theory* as a topic of architectural pedagogy and adopt instead a term—such as "architectural discourse" or even "architectural rhetoric"—that has been less subject to abuse.

This abuse is two-sided: on the one hand, "theory" has come to suggest an abstruse, erudite form of presentation which serves as a tool of intellectual one-upmanship, often (but not always) wielded by either PhD-holding academics or architects trained at elite schools. On the other hand, "architectural theory" suggests the assertion of a defensive (or offensive) position which helps transpose design work into the domain of academic discussion. This kind of theory functions through a network of allusive terms signifying "academic discourse," allowing designs that are largely empty of research or interrogative intellectual content to be presented as a form of scholarship.

The fact that theory bears these connotations has something to do with the continuing prevalence of attitudes associated with the anti-Marxian "postcritical" turn first articulated in schools of architecture around the dawn of the 21st century.[1] This essay will point out some troubling pedagogical ramifications of these versions of architectural theory, versions that endeavor to arrange the world into belligerently opposing camps, often relying on specious jingoism. This is certainly not to suggest that every presentation assignable to the category of architectural theory is corrupted by such tendencies but rather to argue for a reconsideration of the pedagogical usage and discursive arrangement of the term *theory*, in light of how its usage has recently come to support neoliberal politics, whether or not explicitly identified as "postcritical."

Symptomatic of the 21st century's postcritical turn (even if ambivalently so) was a satirical short film, *Notes for those Beginning the Discipline of Architecture*, produced more than a decade ago by the architect and educator Michael Meredith.[2] In the film, Meredith played the role of an architect invited to partake in a public conversation

---

1 A postcritical position (or attitude) has been articulated by many, most notably Michael Speaks who has authored many articles hewing to the basic tone of postcritical theory, including a series of multiple articles on "Design Intelligence" published in A+U: Architecture and Urbanism, beginning in 2002. See also Speaks, "Intelligence after Theory," Perspecta 31, no. 1 (January 2006): 101–106; Speaks, "Design Intelligence and the New Economy," Architectural Record 190, no. 1 (January 2002): 72–76. See also essays by Robert Somol and Sarah Whiting whose "projective architecture" is a byword for postcritical: Robert Somol and Sarah Whiting, "Notes around the Doppler Effect and Other Moods," Perspecta 33, no. 1 (January 2002): 72–77; and Robert Somol and Sarah Whiting, "Okay, Here's the Plan...," Log 5 (Spring/Summer 2005): 4–7.

2 Michael Meredith, David Fenster, David Nordstrom, and Jaron Lubin, Notes for those Beginning the Discipline of Architecture (film), n.d. (c. 2006).

hosted by a daunting architectural theorist who is sneering, bombastic, and perfectly poised.[3] The host's outfit places him in the mid-1970s, alluding to the rise of professionalized architectural theory in the United States during that period. Blonde, mustached, and broad shouldered in his form-fitting jacket, he intellectually bludgeons his architect-guest who sits stoop-shouldered (in a neck-brace, no less), tongue-tied, and hapless. His stammering replies are silenced by the theorist's interjections, circumlocutions, and recondite allusions to literary theorists. Essentially, the theorist emasculates the architect, the film thus offering a comical (and highly gendered) version of a complaint often voiced by architects: that their profession has been gradually rendered impotent by the 1970s rise of academic architectural theory. Implicit to the film's message is an assumption typically proffered by advocates of postcritical theory: namely, that theoretical critique is an annihilative exercise, intent on extinguishing the profession's creativity (an assumption that has itself been persuasively critiqued by Felicity Scott, George Baird, and Reinhold Martin, among others).[4]

That being said, the film's satirical wit opens up other possible interpretations. A generous viewing might regard the film as a commentary on the decreasing tenurability of professional architectural work within universities' research-oriented and finance-driven agenda. (But, in that case, why take on the bogeyman of "theory" instead of universities' support of the lucrative technosciences?) Another interpretation might regard the representation of one hyper-masculine white male establishing his dominance over another as an ironic parody of how hegemonic power-structures remain largely intact in many architecture schools despite the late-20th-century rise of left-leaning theory at those same schools. This generous interpretation of the film is probably unfounded but it is difficult to say definitively, given the role of

3 The film role is not explicitly called out as that of an architectural theorist or art critic, but the topics and authors the actor alludes to – including Manfredo Tafuri, Peter Berger, and Viktor Shklovsky – suggest this occupation.

4 See Felicity Scott, "Involuntary Prisoners of Architecture," October 106 (Autumn 2003): 75–101. See also George Baird, "'Criticality' and Its Discontents," Harvard Design Magazine 21 (Fall/Winter 2004), http://www.harvarddesignmagazine.org/issues/21/criticality-and-its-discontents; Reinhold Martin, "Critical of What? Toward a Utopian Realism," in The New Architectural Pragmatism, ed. William S. Saunders (Minneapolis: University of Minnesota Press, 2007); and Daniel Barber, "Militant Architecture: Destabilising Architecture's Disciplinarity," The Journal of Architecture 10, no. 3 (2005): 245–253.

irony in the film, which reflects the role irony has assumed in architectural discourse more generally. Irony deliberately obfuscates the distinction between critique and cynical acceptance. Ultimately, Meredith's film remains ambivalently symptomatic (more than critical) of a widespread tendency to scapegoat architectural "theory" for problems that in fact run much deeper, problems tied to higher education's (and architecture's) support of structural inequalities.

Notes for Those Beginning also serves to illustrate my second claim about the abuse of the term *theory* in architectural discourse. The host's intellectual pugilism points to the frequent conflation of "theory" with garrulous "argument." By "argument" I refer to a form of discourse distinct from dialectical reasoning, insofar as it promotes the sense that truth lies squarely with one of two contending camps. This corruption of dialectical critique—dialectic's devolution into argument—is prefigured by the journal title *Oppositions,* a journal tacitly implicated in the film. Although the journal was founded in the spirit of Frankfurt-School theory (a spirit upheld by many editors and contributors), the academic culture spawned by the journal often perversely conveys a sense of theory as embattled polemics rather than as a mode of resisting the tidy resolution of things into unequivocal oppositions. Theory *qua* argument is nowadays encouraged in various ways in architecture schools: first, by syllabi and historical narratives structured as a series of disputes or reactions (e.g., the Whites vs. the Greys; Team Ten against CIAM; practice against theory); second, by the curating of round-table discussions to include *either* a wholly unanimous group *or* a strongly bifurcated group tasked with the spectacle of dueling it out; and thirdly, as I'll show with a personal anecdote, through a pedagogy that compels students to articulate a strong "position," an assertive claim posited without evidence, which is not the same as encouraging students to thoughtfully interrogate complex issues of environmental and/or social justice. What I'm saying is that theory often finds itself not in the boudoir so much as the boxing ring.[5]

---

5 I'm alluding to Manfredo Tafuri's suggestion that postmodernist architectural theory was merely the frivolous talk of the "boudoir." See Tafuri, *The Sphere and the Labyrinth: Avant-Gardes and Architecture from Piranesi to the 1970s* (Cambridge, Massachusetts: MIT Press, 1987 [1980]), trans.

MAY '68 (OR WHAT COUNTS AS THEORY)

The professionalization of architectural theory has been linked to the origin myth of May '68, a myth encoded in many course rubrics offering post-'68 architecture theory courses, as well as in K. Michael Hays's edited tome, *Architecture Theory since 1968,* an anthology largely drawn from a circle of academics associated with *Oppositions* and New York's Institute of Architecture and Urban Studies.[6] Granted, the events of May '68 had some influence on the left-leaning strains of late 20th-century Euro-American architectural discourse. That being said, *other* events also influenced those tendencies—for example, earlier moments in the United States' civil rights movement and related decolonization movements in Asia and Africa; or, on the other hand, the economic recessions of the 1970s spurred on by the geopolitics of petroleum, which resulted in high unemployment for architects. Moreover, much of the late 20th-century architectural discourse included in such courses ranges between highly conservative to ambivalently leftist. The emphasis on May '68 risks concealing the continuing domination of architectural canons by the capitalist agenda and by elite-educated white men. (This is notwithstanding the importance of several feminist authors and architects within the *Oppositions* circle, but it is telling that Hays's anthology sometimes stresses their internecine battles more than their shared feminist project).[7]

At worst, the allusion to radical politics can provide an alibi for maintaining the *status quo* of who gets to theorize on behalf of whom. For example, we could consider the critical reception around the famous 1970 International Design Conference at Aspen (IDCA) themed on the topic of "Environment by Design." Seen as a radical moment of reckoning in architectural discourse, the conference came under siege by environmental activists who descended upon Aspen to protest the conference's conservative and superficial treatment of environmental

---

Pellegrino d'Aciemo and Robert Connolly: Ch. 8 "*Architecture dans le boudoir.*"

6 K. Michael Hays, ed., *Architecture Theory since 1968* (Cambridge, Massachusetts: MIT Press, 1998).

7 Of the small handful of female authors included in Hays' anthology, several were engaged in feminist discourse. However, only one contribution in the anthology clearly deals with feminism (see Jennifer Bloomer, "Abodes of Theory and Flesh: Tabbles of Bower" in Hays, ed., *Architecture Theory*). On the other hand, the piece Hays includes by Beatriz Colomina, well-known for her contribution to feminist architectural discourse, is framed by Hays as an argument between Colomina, Mary Macleod, and Joan Ockman.

politics.[8] Dissent was also voiced by invited conference speakers such as Jean Baudrillard's "French Group," which denounced mainstream environmentalist propaganda as a distraction from imperialist wars in Southeast Asia. The efforts of the French Group and the student protesters have, with good reason, been regarded as an important challenge to the architectural profession.[9] Yet Baudrillard's role as the heroic "trojan horse" of the conference has strangely overshadowed a still more revolutionary event, namely the talk delivered by Cora Walker, an African-American lawyer and community activist.[10]

Walker described how she and her collaborators had successfully challenged slum clearance projects in Harlem, working with local residents to implement alternative forms of urban investment, ultimately introducing a much-needed grocery store, low-cost low-rise housing, job training programs, and skilled jobs.[11] Walker prefaced this account with a few incisive criticisms of the conference, noting that its roster of corporate sponsors (including from the extractive petroleum and mining industries) cast aspersions on the organizers' professed commitment to the environment. She also alluded to the fact that environmental degradation disproportionately affected poor black neighborhoods—an observation that suggested a theoretical reevaluation of the contours of environmental politics. The novelty of Walker's inclusion at the IDCA and the impressiveness of her contribution rendered her subsequent

---

8 On the 1970 IDCA, see Jean-Louis Voileau, "Jean Baudrillard, 68 et la *fonction utopique,*" *Laboratoire Urbanisme Insurrectionel,* June, 2012, http://laboratoireurbanismeinsurrectionnel.blogspot.fr/2012/06/baudrillard-68-et-la-fonction-utopique.html; Anon. "Aspen 1970. Conversation avec Martin Beck," *Rosa B* 5 "The Environment by Design"; Alice Twemlow, "'A Guaranteed Communications Failure,' Consensus Meets Conflict at the International Design Conference in Aspen, 1970," in *The Aspen Complex,* ed. Martin Beck (Berlin: Sternberg Press, 2012); Alice Twemlow, "I can't talk to you if you say that: An ideological collision at the International Design Conference at Aspen, 1970," *Design and Culture* 1, no. 1 (2009): 23–49; and Alice Twemlow, "A Look Back at Aspen, 1970," August 28, 2008, *The Design Observer Group,* http://designobserver.com/feature/a-look-back-at-aspen-1970/7277.

9 Reyner Banham omitted Walker's contribution in his publication of the conference proceedings. See Banham, ed., *The Aspen Papers: Twenty Years of Design Theory from the International Design Conference in Aspen* (New York: Praeger, 1974).

10 Cora Walker, conference proceedings for the 20th International Design Conference. International Design Conference in Aspen papers, Special Collections and University Archives (Box 11, Folder 576), University of Illinois at Chicago.

11 Ibid.

exclusion from contemporaneous and historical assessments of the event—including omission from a book publication of the conference proceedings—all the more striking.

It would be wrong to see Walker's blackness and femaleness as causes *in themselves* for this exclusion (given that most postmortems on the event are sympathetic to civil rights and feminist politics).[12] However, Walker's talk comes to us in a form that the architectural academy would not readily recognize as "theory." First of all, Walker was neither an author nor an academic, and therefore not easily consignable to a particular academic movement such as postmodernism or poststructuralism. Her talk did not perform a dramatic gesture of unmasking the hidden truth of things (as the French Group's did). To include Walker's contribution within a canon of architectural theory would require reevaluating the spectacular quality and accepted narrative structure of much theoretical work, as well as, on the other side of the spectrum, the easy jingoism of many architects' texts. Nowadays, in a theater of architectural discourse which increasingly belongs to a hyper-competitive marketplace, aesthetic aplomb and a penchant for raising provocative-sounding questions (as satirized by Meredith's host) sometimes confers more market value than sober interrogation and positive action of the sort carried out by Walker and her colleagues.

It is for these reasons I suggest that the term "theory" may have outlived its usefulness as a pedagogic category for describing architectural discourse. Teaching architectural *discourse* would instead ideally focus on identifying the methods, terms, and thematic orientations that would allow contributions such as Walker's to be conceived as worthy of pedagogic attention. Conversely, a focus on architectural *rhetoric* would draw attention to the values, categories, and terms through which such contributions have been excluded from architectural compendia. It should be stressed that this proposal supports rather than retracts the inclusion of many texts from other disciplines typically canonized as theory, such as Edward Said's *Orientalism.* Indeed, the fact that many authors called "theorists" hail from demographic groups underrepresented in Euro-American academia might have to do with the nature of theoretical interrogation. When one's academic authority is not supported by birthright within a dominant group, there is greater impetus to question the terms and categories through which domination is enacted and authorized. At any

12 See essays in Beck, *The Aspen Complex.*

rate, the prevalence of female authors and authors of color writing theories in many other disciplines makes the architectural canon's lack of such diversity seem especially suspect. My hypothesis is that this lack of diversity is related to the entanglements between "postcritical" discourse and what often passes for "theory" in schools of architecture —which often tends toward blunt assertion, mystique, and combat.

WHEN STUDENTS REINVENT JIM CROW

Why does the discipline of architecture so often privilege antagonism? Perhaps because antagonism conveys the illusion that the stakes *must be* worth fighting for. In other words, in configuring the boudoir as a boxing ring, architects are relieved from a mounting sense of professional "impotence." By staging one's consensual complicity with capitalism as a risky and polemic move (i.e., a daring rejection of Marxian theory), one's resignation is cast as positive action. In this sense, "theorists" are an easy scapegoat for much more real threats posed to architectural labor, as the profession becomes narrowly circumscribed in specialized fields and beholden to real estate developers, engineers, entertainment industries, and product developers. What is endangered by attacking critical theory is not the status of critical theory (which is given relevance by being attacked), but rather the status of architectural practice, as many educators and practitioners refuse to confront the profession's incremental divestment of its more utopian ambitions. Argument (in lieu of what is considered theory in the humanities and social sciences) often serves to academically and professionally legitimize the negation of utopian aspirations. This task is often thrust upon young students.

In 2013 I served as a midterm review critic for an MArch studio that had students design an indoor swimming pool on a small unbuilt tract of land belonging to a public housing complex in Harlem. The "client" for the project was Columbia University. The studio teacher required her students to read to the reviewers a one-page statement, asserting a cogent "argument" (her term), presumably to gild this dismal assignment with a veneer of theoretical sophistication. Under the mandate to justify building a university-owned pool (serving Columbia's mostly affluent students) inside a low-income housing complex, one group of students essentially reinvented Jim Crow. They proposed to have one pool on an upper floor for Columbia affiliates and another below for local residents. The "argument" the students offered to support this introduction of a class-segregated (and largely racially-segregated) building on a public site was to offer a number of architectural contrivances that, they claimed, would *protect* Harlem pool users from the presumed prejudice of Columbia users. The walls and floors of Columbia students' separate pool, entrance, and locker room would afford fleeting glimpses into the local residents' corresponding spaces. These glimpses, the students explained, would be distorted with pixelated and colored glass and sound-distorting techniques, so that, claimed the students, the mostly African-American residents *need not feel ashamed* of how they looked or spoke.

As another reviewer and I struggled to address the implications of this proposal, the teacher abruptly cut us off, loudly defending the proposal on the basis of its concise articulation of what she called an "argument." To interrogate the implications of the students' "argument" was clearly to miss the point, which was not in fact to argue (or, rather, discuss in a civil manner) but to teach students how to legitimize their conscripted involvement in urban expropriation by casting it as an act of intellectual agency. Outlandish and offensive assertions—under the guise of "theory"—took the place of serious intellectual engagement. In other words, one form of violence (against residents of a public housing project) was authorized by an aestheticized translation of violence into the structure of what was called "theory." The studio teacher had recently graduated with accolades from an Ivy-League program with a history-theory requirement consisting of a course called "Arguments." In this teacher's defense, we might demand why the architecture department had assigned the first-year M.Arch cohort a project that used design as a way to justify expropriation. It should be mentioned that, concurrently with this design studio, the university was pursuing a massive expansion into Harlem in the form of a new corporate-office style campus designed by a roster of prestige architects.

This was not the first time Columbia University had proposed large-scale incursions into local neighborhoods. The swimming pool assignment recalled how May '68 had erupted at the university in response to university proposals to build a gymnasium (dubbed "Gym Crow" by local dissenters) on public land in Morningside Park.[13] A rocky escarpment stretching along the Columbia-side of this park has long functioned as a boundary between the university and Harlem. To preempt opposition, the university offered an architectural solution to

13 Technically, the student protests at Columbia took place in April – not May – of 1968. For an account of the events, see Paul Cronin, "Introduction," in *A Time to Stir: Columbia '68*, ed. Paul Cronin (New York: Columbia University Press, 2018), xxxi.

justify expropriation: the building would accommodate on its lower floor, facing Harlem, a small community center for local residents. Calling this out as racial segregation, Columbia's Student Afro-American Society (SAS) joined forces with campus anti-war protesters. The SAS's activities led finally to the university's abdication of the project.[14]

Given this history, it came as a sharp surprise to witness a Columbia design instructor's defense of a renewed version of "Gym Crow," and how this defense relied on a neoliberal version of architectural theory that often disingenuously invokes May '68 as part of its fanciful origin myth. The students' repetition of Gym Crow—proposed under the duress of having to "theorize"—illuminates a problem endemic to many architecture-school curricula, which is to separate out history courses from theory courses. Studying local *histories* of 1968, along with theories supposedly spawned by its events, might have prevented students' reinvention of Gym Crow. This unfortunate episode of design pedagogy offers a lesson: that rather than perpetuating yet another spurious argument—one that perhaps pits architectural practitioners against PhD-holding historian-theorists—architectural education might be better served by a collaborative confrontation of the problems posed by the neoliberalization of higher education. We teachers might collectively interrogate the ways we are asked to serve as apologists-*cum*-theorists for the power-structures undergirding today's universities. •

---

14 For further history, see essays in *A Time to Stir* including William W. Sales, Jr., "Self-Determination and Self-Respect: Hamilton Hall, Fifty Years Later," 300–308.

Schooling Theory

Joseph Bedford

ARCHITECTURAL THEORY WITHIN ARCHITECTURE SCHOOLS

Schools of architecture in the Anglo-American world have become principal sites for the reproduction of theoretical work in architecture ever since they became part of research universities. This process was complete in the United States by the mid-20th century, as many of the architecture schools that emerged within training-oriented land-grant universities in the 1860s now found themselves within institutions that had transitioned into some of the world's leading research universities. In the United Kingdom, this process was taking place through the 1950s and 1960s as the pupilage system was phased out and attendance at university-based schools became the sole path to licensure.[1] As the research university expanded in the United States and the United Kingdom in the mid-20th century, it came to play a leading role in the patronage of cultural production, becoming the principal site of creative work for a range of other fields: music, art, literature, theatre, and

---

1 Between 1958 and 1984 the percentage of students qualifying as architects in university schools went from 54 to 97. Mark Crinson and Jules Lubbock, *Architecture: Art or Profession?: Three Hundred Years of Architectural Education in Britain* (Manchester: Manchester University Press, 1994), 159.

dance. Architecture was one part of a larger process of the "academicization" of the arts—for good and bad.[2]

It was the entry of architectural education into research universities that in large measure fueled a period of creative energies in schools of architecture, centering new experiments in theoretical work as a driving force in architectural design. Initially the new "theoretical" research produced by architects keen to legitimate their place in the research university was scientific in orientation. Postwar enthusiasm for computation led many architects to produce new (positive) mathematical theories that they hoped would facilitate design methods. Yet, with the cultural revolts of the late 1960s and the opening up of humanities fields like English, Comparative Literature, and French and German studies to the westward migration of continental philosophy—that was kept out of analytic schools of philosophy—the paradigm shifted to a (negative) critical approach to the production of architectural research, conceived as primarily a humanities field.

Despite architectural theory providing a central distinguishing feature of university-based architectural education from the late 1960s to the mid-1990s, it began to decline from the mid-1990s to the present.[3] One can observe this decline in the context of schools themselves by the fact that where theory does appear in architectural theory classes it is now largely taught as a historical survey of past architectural ideas and canonical authors, adopting what Friedrich Nietzsche once criticized, in "On the Uses and Disadvantages of History for Life," as an "antiquarian" and "monumental" mode.[4] Another symptom of a decline

---

2 On the predominant role that the American university came to play in the 1950s and 1960s as a patron of creative work in literature, which argues that something similar applies to most creative fields and to universities in the English-speaking world more generally, see Richard F. Teichgraeber, "Beyond 'Academicization': The Postwar American University and Intellectual History," *Modern Intellectual History* 8, no. 1 (2011), 127–146.

3 Speaking of architectural culture more generally, Michael Speaks has been the most prominent figure to confidently announce the end of theory in architectural culture. See in particular, Michael Speaks, "Theory was interesting... but now we have work: No hope no fear," *Architectural Research Quarterly* 6, no. 3 (September 2002), 209–212, and Michael Speaks, "Intelligence after Theory," *Perspecta* 38 (2006), 101–106.

4 Nietzsche's critical historian brings the past, in his words, "before the tribunal, scrupulously examining it and finally condemning it" in order to "be clear as to how unjust the existence of anything – a privilege, a caste, a dynasty, for example – is, and how greatly this thing deserves to perish. Then its past is regarded critically, then one takes the knife to its roots, then one cruelly tramples over every kind of piety." Friedrich Nietzsche,

in the vitality of theory observed within the current state of theory classes is the conceptualization of theory classes as general education courses in the humanities, in which they are viewed as a compensation or compliment to the otherwise instrumentally-driven and commercially-driven education that dominates the rest of the architecture school. In such a "gen ed" approach, theory classes are either designed to offer skills in so-called "critical thinking," ethics, citizenship, or empathy, or they are designed to offer skills in verbal communication, rhetorical debate, or writing that architects do not commonly receive in studio. Yet such a "gen ed" approach too often misses the disciplinary specificity of what a theory class in a school of architecture should be all about, theories *of* architecture.

What has become absent from the pedagogical site of architectural theory in schools of architecture is thus precisely what Nietzsche, in the same essay, praised as a "critical" mode; one that interprets the past for the sake of the future and is therefore critically engaged with the present.

FOUR CRITICAL CONDITIONS

Four conditions of the present world that one might identify as areas for critical engagement are: 1) the media-technical transformation of our lives, 2) the economic organization of our laboring activities, 3) the urgency of climate change, and 4) the politics of identity.

Firstly, the infinitely hyperlinked and ever-present networks of information that now surround us threaten to degrade our basic ability to think. Temporal and connective boundarylessness produces cognitive fatigue and impairs our ability to construct logical and narrative chains of meaning. The business model of today's information capitalism is based on selling our cognitive attention. It uses systems of behavioral modification that manipulate people in order to improve its prediction algorithms. In doing so, this business model degrades our autonomy and exacerbates the psycho-social pressures that are fueling the current crisis of mental health.[5]

"On the Uses and Disadvantages of History for Life," *Untimely Meditations* (Cambridge, UK: Cambridge University Press, 1997), 76.

5 See Shoshana Zuboff, *The Age of Surveillance Capitalism: The Fight for a Human Future at the New Frontier of Power* (New York: Public Affairs, 2019) and Jaron Lanier, *Ten Arguments for Deleting Your Social Media Accounts Right Now* (New York: Henry Holt and Company, 2018). For a depiction of the darker consequences of social media on human behavior see Richard Seymour, *The Twittering Machine* (New York: Verso, 2020)

Secondly, our laboring activities are shaped by an economic system and culture of business management that conceptualizes human time and energy as something to be made more productive through calculation, competition, and constant measurement, rather than as something that is an end in itself, or a capacity to be directed towards other, less measurable social goods. The economization of all laboring activities through the monitoring of new digital platforms squeezes human energies dry, as does the categorization of every aspect of our lives as labor-time through the deepening interpenetration of these platforms into social life. At just the same time, the platforms themselves enable wealth to accumulate exponentially for those who govern them, and that growing inequality further exacerbates the inability of the majority of people to secure financial resources and time away from work.

To the third point, we are failing to live within natural limits, and to respond to and mitigate suffering caused by a warming planet. We have adopted patterns of consumption based on fossil fuel extraction that cannot be sustained for much longer, and we have become locked into those patterns of consumption by global ideologies of growth and commodity fetishism. We are also failing to imagine new patterns by which to inhabit the earth, even though some of the changes are technically possible, and would likely be socially and politically more fulfilling. As a result of this impasse between necessity and freedom, there is a mounting sense of crisis and an apocalyptic mood within most Western nations.

Fourthly, in an increasingly pluralized, globalized world produced through entangled colonial histories, we are faced with enduring and intractable questions about who we are as individual beings and social groups, and how to relate to one another socially and politically in peaceful and just relationships. Much of our current difficulty in relating to one another stems from the politics of identity, whose theme of difference crucially serves the ends of social justice, but which at the same time can obstruct the formation of community and political power. While identity is an important historical rallying point for the necessary demands for social justice, and while the differentiation of identities can serve to offer new sites of resistance from hegemonic norms, under capitalism identity and its increasing differentiation can just as easily function as an instrument of political atomization, undermining possibilities of challenging the current economic system, and it can be easily assimilated by marketing culture to become another form of niche lifestyle and consumer choice.

Instead of providing the grounds for critical engagement advanced through theoretical work in schools of architecture, these same four conditions ironically often play a part in the very domestication of the space of theory itself.

The media-technical transformation of our lives clearly pervades the university classroom. There has been a decline in habits and practices of patient, close reading of difficult texts as a result of the new cognitive habits of distraction produced by the hypnotic rhythm of clicks, taps, and swipes in which contemporary subjectivity is immersed. The delimited media-forms of magazines, books, and lectures that once facilitated the concentrated energies around a set of shared concerns have been replaced by a generalized informational network, in which the sense of relevance or pertinence of ideas have been dissolved into an overwhelming stream of novelty.

The economic and organizational underpinnings of universities have played a role in reorganizing the laboring activities of students and faculty alike. The measurement of performance in quantified terms through grades, research assessment frameworks, academic performance metrics, and so on, disincentivizes speculative and risky modes of thought that are less conducive to measurement. Much theoretical work could be said to share something with genres of creative writing or fiction, common to the arts, yet architecture has not yet found a way to legitimate such modes of work as established parts of its university-based research culture, which is otherwise assumed to be based upon a scholarly mode that is largely historical, or upon a scientific mode that is largely material and technical. With the narrowing of the job market for secure positions in universities, graduates from doctoral programs have recently opted for the vocation of the historian over that of the theorist despite applying for positions advertised under the title of "history and theory" or "H/T" positions. One reason for doing so is likely the easier task of aligning that vocation with the research culture of the university. Faculty vocationally adopting the mantle of an architectural theorist are now rare in doctoral education and few doctoral students receive training in something that might be viewed as theoretical work.

The mounting consciousness of climate crisis has led to urgent calls to pragmatic action, adaptation, and the rubric of resilience, rather than fueling the more radical rethinking of the entire economic and political system that is the ultimate cause of the crisis. Too often the rhetoric of urgency mistakes engagement for pragmatic adaptation rather than critical reflection. The question of climate may ultimately be nothing to do with u-values and more to do with cultural values; those concerning how we live. It has more to do with the critical interpretation of the historical relationship between economics, politics, and theology than with the seemingly urgent need to invent new technical means to increase energy efficiency.

Finally, the impact of the politics of identity in the classroom has been to place into question a large body of traditional material that has composed the curriculum of university education in the West. Much of this questioning is essential to critical reflection, but some of it too quickly judges the value of the tradition based on the identity of the author, hastily throwing out figures—such as, for example, Marx, Nietzsche, Freud and Heidegger—who enabled that same critical standpoint. From whichever perspective one approaches intercultural dialogue, one is always interpreting a tradition and a culture that one's own interpretative lens is informed by. Historically, one always stands downstream within the tradition one interprets and, inter-culturally, one always stands in a historically enmeshed relationship which precedes interpretation. Yet too often the question of the historical relationship between identities and intercultural conflict is treated as a tribunal in which the judgement is already known; a stance that short-circuits the very process of interpretation and critique so central to the activity of theory in the classroom.

THEORY AT THE CORE

It may be the case that architectural theory in its most critically engaged orientation is somewhat incompatible with its siting inside a school, inside a curriculum, inside a university. It may be that the university, which once made architectural education such a vibrant space, is now inherently an institutionally conservative realm compared to the mood of urgency and change in society at large. At some historical moments our theoretical frameworks advance more rapidly through social change in the streets than through the patient work of interpretation in the university. Having now entered fully within the university, with fewer bridges outside of it than in the 1970s, architectural education, and the theoretical work developed within architectural education, may have become too conservative.

In the two decades following the events of May '68, when experimentation in architectural theory was at its height, the site of theory could be said to have straddled the boundary between the school and the larger world of practice, extra-academic institutions, and the gallery system, to a larger degree and to have been equally supported from outside of universities. This history, still recent within the living memory of our field, has left to architecture schools a specific form of theory generated by these events, resulting in a conception of theory as a synthetic entity that binds together history, criticism, practice, and the broader cultural horizon with present concerns. This entity was not strictly academic, but born partly of contestation in the streets. And it was not necessarily located in one fixed classroom space within the curriculum, but was a synthetic entity pervading the school; from public lectures and conferences to school journals and studios, and seminars taught by theorists and philosophers.[6] Entire schools were oriented towards a horizon one would call "theoretical" insofar as they were geared towards reflection on questions that were not purely determined by the immediate practical horizon of the profession but set by larger cultural problematics.

In the moment when experimentation in architectural theory was at its height, the core "theory class" was not considered a staple feature of the curriculum. Theory was located in advanced elective seminars taught by visiting theorists and theoretically-minded studio professors. Yet without a position in the core of the curriculum, theory was destined to an ornamental rather than structural role, and could be easily removed under new leadership, as it often was. At the end of the 1990s, a range of theory anthologies clearly signaled the idea that theory needed to be taught at the core of the curriculum, that it now had its own canon.[7] Such core theory classes did not emerge everywhere, but

---

6 In terms of journals, one might think of school-based journals such as *Midgard: Journal of Architectural Theory and Criticism* based at the College of Architecture and Landscape Architecture at the University of Minnesota, launched in 1987; *The Journal of Architectural Theory and Criticism* (Academy Editions, London, 1988); *Avant Garde: Journal of Theory and Criticism in Architecture and the Arts,* based at School of Architecture and Planning, University of Colorado at Denver, launched in 1989; and *Columbia D: Documents of Architectural Theory* based at Columbia University, launched in 1992. In terms of lectures and conferences, one notable example is the "Afterwards: Architecture and Theory Conference" at Columbia University in 1991. In terms of philosophers and theorists teaching studios and seminars, one might think of figures like Catherine Ingraham and Jeff Kipnis who were theorists who taught studios, and John Rajchman, Elizabeth Grosz, and Manuel DeLanda, who were philosophers from other departments who taught advanced theory seminars.

7 On this phenomenon see Sylvia Lavin, "Theory into History; Or, the Will to Anthology," *Journal of the Society of Architectural Historians 58,* no. 3 (September 1999), 494–499. Key anthologies of this period included Neil Leach's *Rethinking Architecture: A Reader in Cultural Theory* (London: Routledge, 1996), which was produced as a reader that he had prepared for teaching

there are many examples in different schools of something that looks like a core "theory class" today.[8]

The effect of this change is double-edged, however. On the one hand it represents an institutionalization of theory which marks a success. Theory, as some commentators have observed, was never well-institutionalized and always operated on an unstable entrepreneurial model, or an "autodidactic horizon."[9] This entrepreneurialism was partly a feature of the hybrid space inside and outside of the school, in offices, in the gallery system, or in institutions outside of the university. In this sense, the schooling of theory marks an institutional success in its arrival at the core. In the UK, theory has already been part of accreditation criteria for a while.[10] In the US, it has been excluded from the accreditation criteria for many years which has until now only described criteria for history, but this is set to change with the 2020 proposed draft of new accreditation criteria, in which "theory" and "disciplinary thought" are proposed as new key terms alongside history, suggesting that hiring policies will continue to favor faculty equipped to teach architectural theory in the future.[11]

---

his own MA course in critical theory at the University of Nottingham in the mid-1990s; Kate Nesbitt, ed., *Theorizing a New Agenda for Architecture: An Anthology of Architectural Theory 1965-1995* (New York: Princeton Architectural Press, 1996) and K. Michael Hay's *Architectural Theory Since 1968*(Cambridge, MA: MIT Press, 1998).

8 See: Princeton University (203, 308), MIT (4.297), Harvard (4121, 4223), Columbia University (A4469), Cornell University (6800), Yale (3012, 3021a, 3022b), University of Pennsylvania (512-001), Pratt Institute (252), McGill (301, 352, 652), The University of Utah (4270), Syracuse (242), Southern California Institute of Architecture (2100), Rice (225/525), University of Southern California (314, 563), NYIT (160, 361), University of Michigan (572), Virginia Tech (4114), Dalhousie University (4112.03), and Marywood University (224). Schools around the world have many of the same courses: The Architectural Association (HTS), University of Auckland (ARCHTC 236).

9 Mark Jarzombek has made a similar point in "The School of Architectural Scandals," *e-flux architecture*, https://www.e-flux.com/architecture/history-theory/225182/the-school-of-architectural-scandals/.

10 The UK ARB criteria for history (GC2) reads: "GC2 The graduate will have knowledge of: 1) the cultural, social and intellectual histories, theories and technologies that influence the design of buildings; 2) the influence of history and theory on the spatial, social, and technological aspects of architecture; 3) the application of appropriate theoretical concepts to studio design projects, demonstrating a reflective and critical approach."

11 Whereas the previous accreditation criteria read: "History and Global Culture: *Understanding* of the parallel and divergent histories of architecture and the cultural norms of a variety of indigenous, vernacular, local, and

The value of this increasing institutionalization is that it gives a permanent core position to something called "theory," which marks the crucial recent historical development through which so many schools have passed. Yet it comes at the price of placing theory in a stagnant, or even defensive posture, separating it from that synthetic nexus through which it emerged and in which it thrives.

Theory needs a core orientation towards critical engagement with the present world, as well as towards practices of historical scholarship. It needs a relationship to rapid change taking place in the streets as well as patient interpretation in the classroom. Theory flourishes when it pervades an entire school, synthesizing what takes place in the history class, in studio, and elsewhere. To conceive of theory as one among many classes taught by specialists—who have by now increasingly become specialists in historical research only—is to miss the fact that the word "theory" can name a school-wide approach to engaging with the world in a critically reflective manner, not one that is exclusively market-driven or pragmatic. The theory class, where it exists, should be celebrated, ideally becoming the space where the school comes most critically alive and where it is pushed to its pedagogical and ideological limits.

In sum, the schooling of architectural theory is both problematic and promising at the same time. Institutionalizing the site of architectural theory exclusively inside schools, and in a fixed location inside the school curriculum as one among many classes, tends to domesticate the critically-engaged orientation of theory. Yet this same institutionalization signals a recognition of the centrality of theory to architectural education, acting as a reminder of a recent history of critical engagement that can still pervade the entire school and flourish, if we as educators enable it to do so. •

---

regional settings in terms of their political, economic, social, ecological, and technological factors," the currently-drafted criteria for 2020 reads: "History and Theory – How does the Program ensure that students understand the history of architecture and disciplinary thought? How does the Program help students understand this in the context of social, cultural, economic and political forces?"

Is Architectural Theory Western?

Joseph Godlewski

Assessing the current state and future of architectural theory is a complicated task. Articulating its role in architectural pedagogy is perhaps even more difficult. A number of questions and competing claims muddy the discursive waters at the outset: has architectural theory exhausted its utility in the discipline, superseded by a "post-critical" paradigm of architectural research and "design thinking"?[1] Has theory's influence waned as more evidence-based and ostensibly more objective historians have displaced its practitioners in the academy?

1 Robert Somol and Sarah Whiting, "Notes around the Doppler Effect and Other Moods of Modernism," *Perspecta* 33 (2002): 72–77; Michael Speaks, "Design Intelligence: Or Thinking after the End of Metaphysics," *Architectural Design* 159 (2002): 4–6.

Conversely, is theory now ubiquitous, somehow ingrained in the everyday practices of contemporary designers and architectural thinkers? Has theory fragmented into so many smaller debates that it is now difficult to understand as a coherent practice? Or has it dissolved into other disciplines so much so that it no longer guides discourse in the discipline as it once had? If so, how does one teach a course in architectural theory, particularly in a school of architecture?

In the so-called "Gilded Age of Theory" of the late 1970s and early 1980s, architectural theory occupied a privileged place in the academy, disseminated in renowned journals such as *Oppositions* and *Lotus International*.[2] Architectural theory is actively engaged with poststructuralism, psychoanalysis, and semiotics. Established figures in architecture schools like Peter Eisenman and Bernard Tschumi debated deconstruction with philosopher Jacques Derrida, while also experimenting with their built work in large commissioned projects like the Wexner Center for the Arts and Parc de la Villette. While the language used was often abstract and convoluted, the topics, protagonists, and terms of the discussion were relatively stable. The spirit of inquiry and speculative energy invested in these debates, though not without shortcomings, coalesced into something of a high theory moment for the discipline, inspiring a plethora of written and built work.

The contemporary theoretical landscape is fundamentally different. Theory doesn't hold the esteemed position it once did, and the discipline it acts upon is now much more dissipated. Subverting logocentrism, for example, doesn't seem to be the pressing concern it once was. Moreover, built work that claims to have theoretical merit today tends to take place at a much smaller scale, designed by younger and less established practitioners. Disciplinary boundaries have also liquefied, catalyzing an identity crisis amongst architects, and promoting inwardly-focused analyses of forms of representation, explorations of design "fundamentals" and the project of autonomy, and studies of all things properly "disciplinary."[3] Contributions from geography, anthropology, postcolonial studies, and sustainability discourse have

2 Harry Francis Mallgrave and David J. Goodman, *An Introduction to Architectural Theory: 1968 to the Present* (John Wiley & Sons, 2011), 123.

3 Rem Koolhaas and James Westcott, eds., *Elements: A Series of 15 Books Accompanying the Exhibition Elements of Architecture at the 2014 Venice Architecture Biennale* (Venice: Marsilio, 2014); Pier Vittorio Aureli, *The Project of Autonomy: Politics and Architecture within and against Capitalism* (New York: Princeton Architectural Press, 2008).

challenged our understandings of what constitutes architectural speculation. Add to this questions about the rise of digital media and the fundamentally new ways architects and students access and produce architectural knowledge, and one begins to understand the sense of confusion and disillusionment surrounding the state of architectural theory today.

Despite increased attention to the issues raised above, one condition that remains remarkably underexamined is that architectural theory retains the reputation of being practiced exclusively by Western, usually male subjects. Despite years of debate regarding globalization, identity, and "world systems," Western scholars in Western academies still produce the majority of what is recognized as architectural theory today.[4] The "whiteness of theory"[5] necessarily limits the scope and influence these theories can have on public discourse and our built environment. This dilemma for architectural discourse is made particularly plain in theory anthologies. Anthologies of all stripes are confronted with difficult organizational and editorial questions by definition, but they also provide a sketch of a discipline's values and inevitably influence discourse and what is taught in classrooms. Speaking of literary anthologies, critic Joseph Csicsila argues they provide an "irrefutable record of the academy's changing literary tastes."[6] Examining who and what is chosen to represent architectural theory in the most commonly-used anthologies reveals as much about the discipline's self-image and political unconscious as it does about the individual texts.[7] By calling attention to the identity of the authors most often included in these anthologies, this article argues for a more expansive and inclusive vision of architectural theory beyond its hegemonic white, male, Euro-American history.

From the outset it should be stated that exceptions to this condition exist and progress has been made regarding the diversity of identities contributing to theoretical architectural discourse. The impact that

---

4 Joseph Godlewski, "Global Disciplinary Knowledge," *e-flux architecture*, April 18, 2019, https://www.e-flux.com/architecture/curriculum/260416/global-disciplinary-knowledge/.

5 Ananya Roy, "City Talks: Ananya Roy on Urbanism, Poverty, and the Whiteness of Theory," interview by Hiba Bou Akar and Hun Kim, *Jadaliyya*, May 16, 2016, https://www.jadaliyya.com/Details/33268/City-Talks-Ananya-Roy-on-Urbanism,-Poverty,-and-the-Whiteness-of-Theory.

6 Joseph Csicsila, *Canons by Consensus: Critical Trends and American Literature Anthologies* (Tuscaloosa: University of Alabama Press, 2016).

7 Fredric Jameson, *The Political Unconscious: Narrative as a Socially Symbolic Act* (London: Methuen, 1983).

feminist and postcolonial perspectives have had on architectural debates in recent decades, for instance, should not be underestimated. What is striking is how often this work is classified as architectural history or criticism, as opposed to theory. Take for example the work of scholars as diverse as Jane Rendell, Vikramaditya Prakash, Sibel Bozdogan, Gwendolyn Wright, and Abidin Kusno. While all engage with theory, they're largely understood as historians of the built environment and are rarely included in volumes dedicated to architectural theory proper. The dominance of certain privileged positionalities in speculative architectural thought is worth noting. Reviewing architectural theory literature, both ancient and contemporary, raises the suggestive question: is architectural theory a uniquely Western construct? Or, put another way, is theory reserved for a particular worldview, which locates progress and critique firmly in the Western philosophical tradition?

Competing claims can be made as to whether it is or is not, but this essay argues that, compared to other fields such as architectural history or urban studies, architectural theory proceeds unreflexively as though it is a uniquely Western phenomenon. The reasons for this situation are culturally and epistemologically complex, but theory's Euro-American bias is inarguable and deeply problematic, resulting from the demographics of theory's protagonists, its assumed geographies, and its choice of topics. Drawing attention to this should not undervalue the contributions scholars from historically unrepresented groups have made to the theoretical canon. It should also not be construed as a counter-theoretical movement or an exercise in political correctness or cynical tokenism. Instead, I contend truly globalizing architectural theory can fundamentally challenge our conception of what theory is and what it should do. Architectural theory's present exclusivist position threatens to undermine its very legitimacy as a field of inquiry. It is time architectural theorists learn from related fields, recognize the limitations of their tacit assumptions, and expand how and who conceptualizes theory. I recognize the irony in making this argument as a male scholar in an American publication; however, as I will elaborate, the call for globalizing theory is one that must be made if the act of theorizing is to have any legitimacy now or in the future.[8]

---

8 This argument can be said to build on two earlier essays. Sibel Bozdogan reflected on postcolonial challenges to the history survey in "Architectural History in Professional Education: Reflections on Postcolonial Challenges to the Modern Survey," *Journal of Architectural Education* 52, no. 4 (1999): 207–215. Karen Burns performed a similar analysis on architectural theory anthologies with a focus on gender inequities in her essay "A Girl's Own

Adjacent areas of scholarly investigation do not seem to have the same problems that plague architectural theory. Architectural historians and urban theorists tend to better understand the importance of looking beyond Western civilization for conceptual insights and have made concerted efforts to broaden the reach of their respective fields. For decades, they have sought to dislocate the Western point of view in their research and recalibrate their conceptual language to address difference, global networks, and flows of knowledge.[9] Contemporary accounts of globalization within architectural history and urban theory emphasize transnational flows of people, capital, and ideas. However, it is important to draw attention to the dominant directionality of flows within these narratives—from the center to the periphery, from the developed global North to the underdeveloped global South, and from West to East. The postcolonial urban theorist Ananya Roy suggests that 21st century theorizations must disrupt and de-center these categories. She argues for "dislocating the Euro-American center of theoretical production; for it is not enough simply to study the cities of the global South as interesting, anomalous, different, and esoteric empirical cases."[10] The center of theory-making must move South in order to recalibrate the geographies of authoritative knowledge. Historically, spaces in the global North have been interpenetrated by those from the global South. Networks of knowledge sharing and global trade, for example, have always intersected and overlapped to create new identities and spatial sensibilities, and peripheral zones in the world system have been sites where new ideas in urban and architectural form were tested. Gwendolyn Wright and Paul Rabinow explicitly referred to these sites as "laboratories" of spatial experimentation.[11] Relying on

---

Adventure: Gender in Contemporary Architectural Theory Anthology," *Journal of Architectural Education* 65, no. 2 (2012): 125–134.

9 See Swati Chattopadhyay, "The Globality of Architectural History," *Journal of the Society of Architectural Historians* 74, no. 4 (2015): 411–415; Abodoumaliq Simone, *For the City yet to Come: Changing African Life in Four Cities* (Duke University Press, 2004); and Jennifer Robinson, *Ordinary Cities: Between Modernity and Development* (Routledge, 2013). Diane Favro made the case for urban history shifting to a more global perspective in "Meaning and Experience: Urban History from Antiquity to the Early Modern Period," *Journal of the Society of Architectural Historians* 58, no. 3 (1999): 364–373.

10 Ananya Roy, "The 21st-Century Metropolis: New Geographies of Theory," *Regional Studies* 43, no. 6 (July 2009): 820.

11 Gwedolyn Wright, *The Politics of Design in French Colonial Urbanism* (Chicago: University of Chicago Press, 1991); Paul Rabinow, *French Modern: Norms and Forms of the Social Environment* (Chicago: University of Chicago Press, 1995).

outmoded theoretical models that ignore these connections and historical insights is inadequate for understanding the interdependent dynamics of global flows and connectivity. Moreover, it is pedagogically insufficient to study these areas in sidebar courses on "non-Western architecture." To do so rehearses orientalist tendencies and miscalculates the diverse ways in which centers and peripheries are, in fact, mutually constituted categories. It is worth noting the irony that architectural theory lags behind architectural history in this regard. If the prime point of distinction between history and theory is theory's anticipatory view and aspiration to project new architectural possibilities, shouldn't it embrace a less parochial worldview?

Architectural historians have already begun the work of dethroning the Western canon as the sole referent for understanding all architecture. Innovative surveys about "global" and "world" architectural history have been providing examples from both Western and non-Western contexts for years. Textbooks have noticeably shifted from the Eurocentric classics such as Bannister Fletcher's *A History of Architecture* to new narratives like Spiro Kostof's *A History of Architecture: Setting and Rituals;* Mark Jarzombek, Francis Ching, and Vikramaditya Prakash's *Global History of Architecture;* and Richard Ingersoll's *World Architecture,* which are just a few of the influential textbooks to benefit from a broader geographic perspective.[12] While these more recent volumes are not without their flaws, they do make a concerted effort to construct a more inclusive narrative and articulate the interdependent and international relationships that have historically constituted our built environment. The global perspective is now standard fare in most survey courses in architectural history worldwide. In part due to these pioneering texts, students studying architectural history implicitly understand the need to make global connections and to learn from a more diverse cast of architectural agents. On the other hand, students of architectural theory are not presented with the urgency of this problem.

Just as history textbooks have evolved to incorporate disparate points of view in recent decades, countless historical monographs and edited volumes have been produced exploring alternative modernities and the relationship between Western and non-Western architectural

---

12 Spiro K. Kostof, *A History of Architecture: Settings and Rituals* (Oxford: Oxford University Press, 1985); Francis D. K. Ching, Mark Jarzombek, and Vikramaditya Prakash, *A Global History of Architecture* (John Wiley & Sons, 2007); and Richard Ingersoll and Spiro Kostof, *World Architecture: A Cross-Cultural History* (Oxford: Oxford University Press, 2013).

practices. Countless architectural and urban histories have been influenced by insights from postcolonial theory.[13] Histories of architecture from Asian, South Asian, African, and South American contexts, for example, have challenged singular narratives of modernity. What the postcolonial critiques in these volumes share is the objective of expanding, enriching, and renewing this narrative from the margins.[14] Consider Duanfang Lu's edited volume *Third World Modernism*.[15] In her introduction, she succinctly makes the case for examining spatial logics beyond the Western canon:

> It is important to recognize not only the histories of different modernities, but also the legitimacies of different knowledges . . . It is time to enfranchise other spatial rationalities and architectural knowledges to create a more sustainable, just, and culturally and ecologically rich world. And it is time to open our architectural education to a multi-logical program that encourages mutual persuasions amongst different understandings of dwelling and building.[16]

In her view, it is necessary to understand these intertwined histories in order to unhinge latent assumptions in diffusionist models of modernity and imagine a more equitable and sustainable world.

Compared to these developments in architectural history, architectural theory volumes seem strikingly conservative. Anthologies of architectural theory have been stubbornly resistant to change, and overwhelmingly reliant on texts from the vantage point of white, male, Western authors; for instance, the seminal volumes by Hanno-Walter Kruft, K. Michael Hays, Harry Francis Mallgrave, and A. Krista Sykes.[17]

---

13 For a critical overview of authors who have contributed to postcolonial theories in architecture see Esra Akcan. "Postcolonial Theories in Architecture," in *A Critical History of Contemporary Architecture (1960-2010)* (London: Ashgate, 2014), 115–138, and Jyoti Hosagrahar, "Interrogating Difference: Postcolonial Perspectives in Architecture and Urbanism," in *The SAGE Handbook of Architectural Theory*, eds. C. Greig Crysler, Stephen Cairns, and Hilde Heynen (London: SAGE Publications, 2012), 70–84.

14 Jyoti Hosagrahar, "Interrogating Difference," 83.

15 Duanfang Lu, ed., *Third World Modernism: Architecture, Development and Identity* (Routledge, 2010).

16 Ibid., 25.

17 Hanno-Walter Kruft, *History of Architectural Theory* (New York: Princeton Architectural Press, 1994); K. Michael Hays, ed., *Architecture Theory Since 1968* (Cambridge, MA: MIT Press, 2000), Harry Francis Mallgrave, ed.,

This is particularly concerning since anthologies are often students' first introduction to the world of architectural theory. Sylvia Lavin's now familiar critique that theory anthologies tend to establish a sense of continuity and "lend stability to an otherwise promiscuous body of material" is pertinent and worth noting but overlooks the pedagogical pragmatics of collecting relevant material for students of theory and the legitimating role these collections have. More important for this study, they tend to overlook key contributions from thinkers in large swathes of the world and the multiplicitous feedback loops that exist between cultures.

A closer reading of theory anthologies can illuminate the obstacles to improving this situation. Hanno-Walter Kruft admits in his introduction that the subject of his text is Western architectural theory.[18] He subsequently writes a history from Vitruvius to the end of the 20th century without including a single female voice. The two-volume anthology edited by Harry Francis Mallgrave and Christina Contandriopoulos collects excerpts from an impressive array of architectural texts from 25 BCE to 2005. Though an elusive task, it could be said this collection in its sheer scope best represents what might be understood as the canon of architectural theory. It is striking to note that of the 555 writings represented in these two volumes, only twelve (about two percent) are authored or co-authored by women and only seven (about one percent) are written or co-written by authors from non-Western contexts. There are no black authors included in these volumes. Though the editors apologize in the preface to those who "may feel slighted by [their] limited choice of texts,"[19] the facts raise important questions about who has been permitted to occupy the privileged position of architectural theorist and who has been excluded. Is this lack of representation simply due to lack of space in the anthology or is this structural inequity more telling of what and why we speculate about architecture? Of course, this type of analysis assumes a rather binary (male/female, West/non-West, white/black) sense of identity that should itself be challenged. The point of examining theory anthologies from this perspective is to bring attention to the fact that the "who" of

---

Architectural Theory: Volume I-An Anthology from Vitruvius to 1870 (Wiley-Blackwell, 2005); Harry Francis Mallgrave and Christina Contandriopoulos, eds., *Architectural Theory: Volume II-An Anthology from 1871 to 2005* (Wiley-Blackwell, 2008); and A. Krista Sykes, ed., *Constructing a New Agenda: Architectural Theory 1993-2009* (New York: Princeton Architectural Press, 2010).

18 Kruft, *History of Architectural Theory*, 19.

19 Mallgrave and Contandriopoulos, *Architectural Theory: Volume II*, xxviii.

theory tends to reinforce existing representational inequities.

The influential and often-cited K. Michael Hays anthology performs a bit better in the face of this kind of quantitative, identity-based analysis, but is still symptomatic of a general trend in theory discourse. *Architecture Theory since 1968* includes forty-seven texts and discussions of eleven influential built and unbuilt architectural projects. Of the forty-seven entries, six are by women authors (thirteen percent) and four (nine percent) are from non-Western thinkers, all of whom are from Central or South America. None of the writers are black. All eleven of the projects discussed are by white European or American men. Despite espousing the unprecedented transformations and "radical heterogeneity" in architectural discourse in the later part of the 20th century, the book doesn't present the most inspiring view of an inclusionary politics.[20] Like Mallgrave and Contandriopoulos, Hays acknowledges leaving out important changes in architectural theory, notably developments in feminism and identity politics.[21] The more recent anthology edited by A. Krista Sykes (considered a sequel to Hays' volume) shows modest improvement regarding the diversity of its contributors. Of the twenty-nine texts in *Constructing A New Agenda: Architecture Theory 1993-2009*, six (twenty-one percent) of the entries are authored or co-authored by women and three (ten percent) are authored or co-authored by non-Western thinkers. Again, no black authors are included in this volume. In the book's afterword, Hays argues the selections "exploit the more global reach of a particular commitment, vision, and theory."[22] While a step forward, it is interesting to note that the volume doesn't reflect the "massive numbers of studies" in feminism and identity politics since 1993 he mentioned in his anthology.[23]

The point of this exercise is to call attention to the "who" of architectural theory. Historically, who has speculated about the built environment and who has changed the ways in which we conceive architecture? In the prior examples, Lina Bo Bardi, Arata Isozaki, Charles Correa, Mabel Wilson, Craig Wilkens, and Teddy Cruz, for example, are not considered part of theory's meta-narrative, nor are *The Yingzao Fashi* or Hindu vastu shastras. Such a vantage point is no longer sustainable in today's interconnected world and increasingly diverse architectural

---

20 Hays, *Architecture Theory Since 1968*, 89.

21 Ibid., xiv.

22 K. Michael Hays, "Afterword," in *Constructing a New Agenda: Architectural Theory 1993-2009*, ed. A. Krista Sykes (New York: Princeton Architectural Press, 2010), 475.

23 Hays, *Architecture Theory Since 1968*, xv.

academy and profession. One notable and hopeful exception to the exclusionary tendency is the *SAGE Handbook of Architectural Theory,* which includes literature review essays by a diverse cast of contributors addressing pressing architectural issues with global implications, such as power and difference, technology and virtuality, and ecology and sustainability.[24] The editors state they "believe that theory must be open to continuous revision and change if it is to represent and intervene in the relationship between the built environment and the changing conditions of the world at large."[25] But despite the rare counterexample, much work is needed to mend the perception that architectural theory is an activity confined to certain geographies and practiced by a select few.

Launched in 2017, K. Michael Hays' online, open-source edX course "The Architectural Imagination" offers the exciting possibility of disseminating theoretical discourse to a global audience. It is well-produced, sharply delivered, and innovative in its use of digital media. While this is Hays's clearest exposition of the project of architectural autonomy, it still relies heavily on material positioned within a narrow bandwidth of architectural thinkers from the Euro-American canon.[26] The unqualified title of the course suggests "the architectural imagination" is a world constructed exclusively by white Western men. The authorities are the same as they were when this narrative was prevalent in the 1980s—Alberti, Loos, Rossi, Eisenman, and all the usual suspects. It is striking how uncritically the course embraces these authors and their works. Has nothing changed in the ensuing years to prompt reevaluation?

Hays once offered this definition of architectural theory: "Theory is a practice explicitly ready to undertake its self-critique and effect its own transformation. And, like architecture itself, theory is an appetite for modifying and expanding reality, a desire to organize a new vision of a

---

24 C. Greig Crysler, Stephen Cairns, and Hilde Heynen, eds., *The SAGE Handbook of Architectural Theory* (London: SAGE Publications, 2012).

25 Crysler et al., *The SAGE Handbook of Architectural Theory,* 17.

26 For similar critiques of "The Architectural Imagination" and the project of autonomy see Kevin Block, "Autonomy Online: A Review of edX's 'The Architectural Imagination,'" in *The Avery Review* 26 (October 2017), http://averyreview.com/issues/26/autonomy-online; Christopher Hawthorne, "Harvard's first online architecture course: Does it make the grade?" in *The Los Angeles Times,* May 4, 2017, https://www.latimes.com/entertainment/arts/la-ca-cm-building-type-harvard-course-20170507-story.html; and Joseph Godlewski, "The Absurd Alibi," *The Plan Journal* (2016): 7–14.

world perceived as unsatisfactory or incomplete."[27] What this new course and many forms of contemporary architectural theory lack, ultimately, is this sense of self-reflexivity, or self-critique. They lack the idea that theory is an open-ended engagement and that it actively responds to changes in the world—sensibilities that are vital for effective theoretical speculation. With the world changing at an incredible pace, architecture will continue to be challenged in unforeseen, existential ways. In order to keep its legitimacy, theory requires much more rigorous strategies to enfranchise other ways of thinking about architecture and alterities that are just coming into being. Not merely the status of architectural theory, but the very ways we understand ourselves and our environment are at stake. ●

27 Hays, *Architecture Theory Since 1968*, xiv.

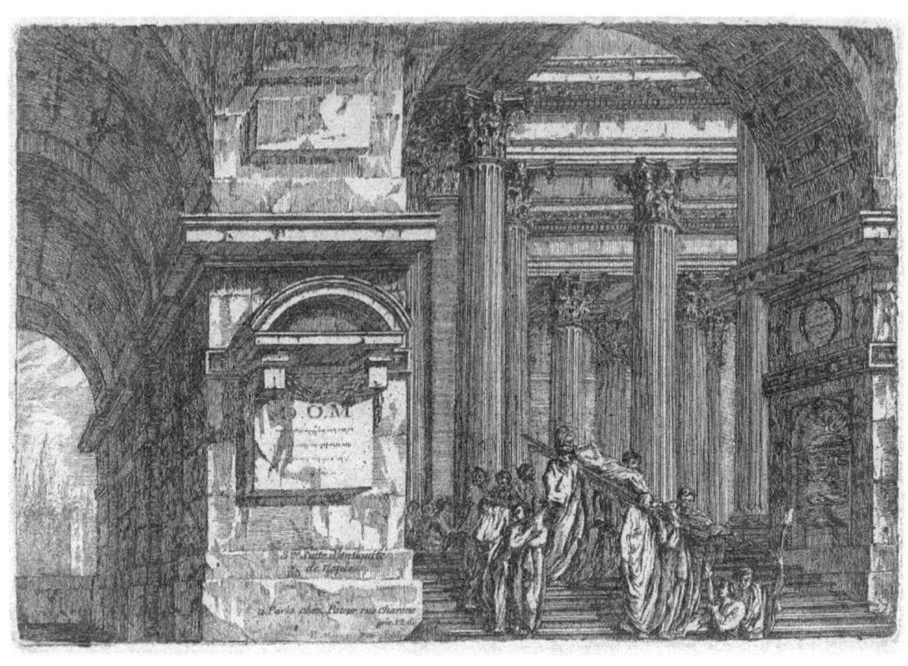

Pierre Moreau, *Funeral Scene in Imaginary Architecture,* undated, etching.
Image credit: National Gallery of Art, https://www.nga.gov/collection/art-object-page.62539.html.

Liquid. The Present of Architecture Theory

Ivonne Santoyo-Orozco

Theory has died a thousand deaths. Within and beyond architecture, many have mourned the 'end of theory.' Whether it is a lament of the waning importance of grand narratives, or a certain frustration about the efficacy of intellectual work, theory's present and future have often been described as uncertain. Depictions of theory's demise abound, from those describing theory as a "ghost unable to find its rest,"[1] to

1 Philip Ursprung, "The End of Theory?", *e-flux architecture*, October 25, 2017, http://www.e-flux.com/architecture/history-theory/159230/the-end-of-theory/.

those presenting it as a "politically impotent" activity.[2] But to lament this is perhaps to misunderstand the practice of the theorist. Or, more precisely, it is to misunderstand theory's relation to the present. At a moment in which our planetary future is uncertain, the urgency to reconsider our tools of analysis and our discursive practices has never been greater.[3] If a "critical interrogation of the present" is not to be conflated with reaction to an instantaneous or passing moment, but instead recognized as an "attitude, an ethos, a philosophical life in which the critique of what we are is at one and the same time the historical analysis of the limits that are imposed on us and an experiment with the possibility of doing beyond them,"[4] as Foucault argues, then a critique of the present reveals itself as a destabilizing force. It might not only generate new openings but, with them, the possibility to transform the present. Perhaps the very act of theory, of actively engaging in discourse, is always an act of doing and undoing, of success and excess—an opening and a closing.

How can theoretical inquiry ever die? Has theory become redundant? For decades, history and theory within architecture have been framed as distinct practices, unspoken enemies undermining each other. Within architecture, this supposed decline of theory, as the final issue of *Assemblage* declared in 2000, coincided with a surge in architectural history scholarship whose historical and geopolitical scope has opened more contentious regions of inquiry that resound in the concerns of the present—histories of colonial subjugation, environmental history, and migration. So, indeed, why do we need theory if it is already implicit in the frame of analysis that much of history now employs? Next to the rigor of history, theory arguably appears as ungrounded, unguided speculations, lacking commitment to historical detail. But perhaps such a view of the field of architectural scholarship is based on a false opposition.

---

2 See the position of Stanley Fish, Sander Gilman, and Henry Louis Gates in W. J. T. Mitchell, "Medium Theory: Preface to the 2003 Critical Inquiry Symposium," *Critical Inquiry* 30, no. 2 (Winter 2004): 324–335.

3 Michel Foucault articulates this relation between philosophical work and the present in the opening lecture of Michel Foucault, *The Government of Self and Others, Lectures at the Collège de France 1982-1983* (New York: Palgrave Macmillan, 2011), 13. For an interpretation of this lecture see Michael Hardt, "The Militancy of Theory," *The South Atlantic Quarterly* 110, no. 1, (Winter 2011): 19.

4 Michel Foucault, "What is Enlightenment?" in *The Foucault Reader*, ed. P. Rabinow (New York: Pantheon Books, 1984), 32–50.

If theory, as Michael Hardt argues, is characterized by a "process of becoming,"[5] then theory has nothing to do with dismissing the past, but instead constantly mobilizes it. Theory, in this way, remains actively committed to the construction of the multiple histories that constitute the present. Yet, this is not only an account of what theory has been, but also an argumentative opening toward alternative ways of seeing what theory could be. Unavoidably, theory cannot do it alone. Just as facts without critical analysis have little to say in and of themselves, theory without history is inconsequential, and archives without argument have little consequences beyond architecture. So, rather than enforcing unproductive oppositions, or looking nostalgically to the glory that theory has putatively lost, or declaring, as many have done, that "architecture today is in an a-theoretical phase,"[6] here I would like to advocate for a more fluid relationship between architecture history and theory—between the past and its multiple openings and the present and its situated and propositional narratives.

To think in this way is to retreat from the idea that theory is a unified, solid, and enclosed corpus of writing relevant to architecture. It is to refuse a stable canon. Because "the death" of theory implies a singularity, it seems to treat theory as a body that lives or dies, a body that becomes allergic to the grand narratives, a body that can be healed at the nearest art gallery bookshop, a body that speaks one language. But theory is not a singular entity, nor a unified form of inquiry; rather, it is a process of interrogating, situating, and unsettling the present. Theory is not a thing that can be applied to a given body of evidence, but an active way of thinking that challenges the present. To practice it, one must first take a position. In doing so, we might shamelessly embrace a plurality of theoretical inquiry, multiple forms of discerning the relevant histories that illuminate the present. To engage in theory along these lines is not to do history, or to do theory, or history-and-theory, or history-of-theory, but instead to be concerned with a present that matters.

> *"It would be better for theory to divert itself, than to be diverted from itself."*[7]
> *–Jean Baudrillard*

---

5 Hardt, "The Militancy of Theory," 21.

6 Philip Ursprung, "The End of Theory?".

7 Jean Baudrillard, "Why Theory?", *The Ecstasy of Communication* (Los Angeles: Semiotex(e), 2012), 100.

To reflect on this proposition, I would like to consider the practice and content of theory as *liquid*. To imagine theory as a liquid speaks to the challenge of containing the present. Liquids are never stable. They disperse, evaporate, separate, and become amorphous, but they also have a force. As it flows, liquid has the capacity to disturb, to divert from its course, to carve, shape, destabilize, and to violently destroy. To think along these lines involves not only situating theory in relation to an always-precarious present, but also alongside its potential transformation. In other words, every time theory attempts to act as a constitutive force, in its attempts of becoming it also always bears the potential to be destructive. And, yet, to call the practice of theory liquid is also to confront its paradoxical character. Liquid is easily affected by externalities: its amorphous appearance is precisely a mapping of its relations to and penetrations by that which comes into contact with it. To think with this metaphor is to re-situate theory as an active agent, being contaminated by other discourses just as it redefines them and, in doing so, potentially reimagining disciplinary norms. It is not only about a response to the present, but about constituting it in the first place.

For this reason, to refer to the practice of the theorist as liquid should not be confused with an anything-goes, value-free attitude—which has certainly characterized many architectural theories of the recent past. It is instead a call to resist passive flows, movement, or evaporation. It is an attempt to capture the precarity of the present: to contain it, if only for a moment, in order to make it legible. To do this, the theorist must act with a certain militant attitude. She or he must articulate a discourse that flows with its own force, rather than one that lets other forces define its course, and bring about a discourse that matters in the present, that constitutes and destroys. For this, the theorist requires an aggressive political attitude.

> *"There is nothing softer and weaker than water. And, yet, there is nothing better for attacking hard and strong things."*[8]
> *–Laozi*

For Hardt, the militancy of theory can only exist if theory remains critically engaged with the present. For him, the theorist must "understand the locus of theory and the production of knowledge as

---

8 Laozi (debated), *Tao Te Ching (Dao De Jing), The Book of the Way,* Proposition 78 (6th Century BC).

taking place primarily collectively in social struggles."[9] Or, as the Argentinean collective *Situaciones* declares, the position of "the militant-researcher tries to generate a capacity for struggles to read themselves and, consequently, to recapture and disseminate the advances and productions of other social practices."[10] For this reason, theorists must also provide a forum to interpret common struggles. Just as liquid condenses and evaporates, historical forces and movements appear and disappear. In the same way, resonances of the past fade and reemerge in the becoming of the present. As Benjamin reminds us in "On the Concept of History," the past has a claim on the present.[11] Again, rather than trying to identify the present as something that can be named, reduced, or bracketed, I advocate thinking of the present as an understanding of intersections between discourses, practices, and histories that maps out a common struggle today. For this reason, my use of liquid to understand the role of the theorist should not be confused with Zygmunt Bauman's notion of 'liquid modernity,' which he employs to characterize the current stage of modernity.[12] While I share much of his critique, including his understanding of 'fluidity,' I use liquid not to define our times, or a new type of theory, but to show the obsoleteness of disciplinary boundaries. The role of the theorist cannot be confined to naming tendencies that supposedly define the 'now'—an activity which is destined to be consumed in its attempt to provide a narrative that centralizes and singularizes. Instead, it could be about allowing a mode of thinking in architecture to actively *intersect* with other forms of knowledge, practices, and histories that resonate in making a present that matters. The collective *Situaciones* understood this well when they argued that "militant research works neither from its own set of knowledge about the world nor from how things ought to be."[13] But to address this, we must reformulate our questions and confront how our present is embedded in deep histories of colonization and extractive capitalism.

---

9 Hardt, "The Militancy of Theory," 33–34.

10 Colectivo Situaciones, *On the Researcher-Militant*, trans. Sebastian Touza, in *Utopian Pedagogy*, ed. M Coté, R Day, and G Peuter (University of Toronto Press, 2007), 186–200.

11 Walter Benjamin, "On the Concept of History," in *Selected Writings, Volume 4: 1938-1940*, ed. Jennings Eiland (Cambridge, MA: Belknap Press, 2003), 389–400.

12 See Zygmunt Bauman, *Liquid Modernity* (Cambridge, UK: Polity Press, 2000).

13 Colectivo Situaciones, *On the Researcher-Militant*, 186–200.

> *"When metaphor invades decolonization, it kills the very possibility of decolonization; it recenters whiteness, it resettles theory, it extends innocence to the settler, it entertains a settler future."*[14]
> *–Tuck and Yang*

In order to do this, we must first confront how theory is historically situated today. The professionalization of both academia and architectural practice continuously poses obstacles to addressing broader geopolitical questions. Increasingly specialized boundaries are drawn that resist the possibility of capturing architecture's relation to the present, reducing it to treating the present as something to fetishize or commodify. History and theory, commonly lumped together as a region of architectural discourse, in practice often remain separate from one another. As Joan Ockman argues,[15] when the two are coupled it remains unclear how productive or detrimental the tension is that separates the ampersand and the slash. Uncomfortably paired, they seem to shadow the contradictions that remain between academia and practice. Yet, my argument also implies a commitment to reading the past to articulate the present. As Ockman fearlessly argued in the final issue of *Assemblage* in 2000: "There can be no history without theory. There can be no theory without history. History without theory is just one thing after the other. Theory without history is hubris."[16] Indeed, it is not enough to put theory and history into a table of equivalences; the relation between them has to be mobilized by establishing a mode of thinking toward and with the present. In other words, I don't think our diagnosis of the present condition of architectural theory is worthwhile, nor is it useful to situate this in relation to our present interpretations of and attitudes toward 'history'; rather, it is about the way theory always constitutes its own present in relation to the present.

In a present that is neither peaceful nor just, we—those of us engaged in architectural discourse—should ask: for whom should the present of theory be written? At whom do we direct architectural discourse? These are questions that exist beyond our professional comfort zones. They are not of purely epistemological importance; they carry a political urgency. How can architectural discourse grapple with more systemic questions—with the struggles of the dispossessed, with

---

14 Eve Tuck and K Yang, "Decolonization Is Not a Metaphor," *Decolonization: Indigeneity, Education and Society* 1, no. 1 (2012): 3.

15 See Joan Ockman, "Slashed," *e-flux architecture*, October 27, 2017, http://www.e-flux.com/architecture/history-theory/159236/slashed/.

16 Joan Ockman, *Assemblage* 41 (2000): 61.

colonized legacies, with planetary ecologies? More specifically, how can this be possible if, in its Western form, architecture has built itself around notions of private property, colonialism, and the values of capitalism, which are directly antithetical to the struggles of those whose voices are marginalized? Yet it is precisely because architecture is so strongly bound up in the circulation of capital—used as an instrument of racial segregation, demanding massive extraction of resources, mobilizing and disciplining human labor, and reifying regimes of private property—that architectural discourse offers a crucial lens to document spatio-political struggles, and to connect them. This is where history and theory need each other.

Architectural discourse cannot be only about mastering archives or making arguments. It must be about mobilizing each other in order to unsettle architecture itself and the systems that make it possible. This is the zone of discomfort, the state of disciplinary disorder, that we should test in order to move beyond a fragmented discourse that otherwise privileges individuals, enclaves, archives, and objects. We should remember that we are not alone in this epistemological quest, that there are strong precedents. Indigenous knowledge, for example, not only offers a vision of history with a stake in the present—constantly "projecting itself backward and forward in time"[17]—but is also founded in *relationality,* capturing histories, practices, and life-worlds always in relation to larger systems, technologies, and ecologies. As Nick Estes reminds us, we need "theory as a weapon and history as a guide... all knowledge is produced through relationships."[18]

In this respect, perhaps my call to consider architectural discourse as attaining a liquid state is somehow reductive, yet it aims to draw attention to the fact that our tools of analysis are insufficient to grapple with the entanglements of our contemporary spatial reality. Reflecting Estes' reminder of indigenous relationality, it captures a clear mandate that can only exist if we are able to break from our internal divisions and self-enclosed realms of architectural knowledge production. With this call for discursive engagement with our political reality, we could abandon questions such as: what can theory and history do for architecture? Instead, we could use architecture as a lens to contest, confront, and unsettle our pasts, presents, and imaginaries of the future. In this conception, architecture is both a product of and a vehicle for the

17 Nick Estes, *Our History Is the Future: Standing Rock Versus the Dakota Access Pipeline, and the Long Tradition of Indigenous Resistance* (London: Verso Books, 2019), 18.
18 Ibid., 259.

intersections that constitute and illuminate any particular present over another. It is for anyone engaged in our political reality to make legible the different discourses, forces, and practices that contact one another, to embrace the heterogeneity of practicing a theory that intersects multiple histories. And, it is for those engaged in architectural discourse to imagine an engagement with the production of knowledge that challenges disciplinary common sense—the set of presuppositions and presumptions that foregrounds the questions that matter and ignores those that do not.

> *"How can we marry our thought so that we can now pose the questions whose answers can resolve the plight of the Jobless archipelagoes, the NHI categories, and the environment?"*[19]
> *–Sylvia Wynter*

Turning our discourse toward Wynter's question involves not only thinking about architecture as a relational field of inquiry, but also continually questioning our production of knowledge and its self-imposed hierarchies. Perhaps, today, this is a distant disciplinary fantasy, but to do so is to imagine *unsettling architecture's common sense.*[20] Perhaps failing to do so is the same as operating within the disciplinary confines established twenty years ago, where theory was thought to be 'dead.' In confronting how we produce knowledge, we might ask instead: what are the present collective struggles? What are we fighting for or against? Under conditions of hyper-individualization, perhaps the greatest challenge is to shift the questions from the I, the you, and the yours, to the we, the us, and the ours. ●

19 Sylvia Wynter, "No Humans Involved. An Open Letter to My Colleagues," *Forum NHI Knowledge for the 21st Century* 1, no. 1 (1994): 65.

20 This argument of "unsettling architecture's common-sense" draws from my ongoing work on pedagogy with Ross Exo Adams.

Theory Now

Jake Matatyaou

THINKING THEORY

Theory stands for a certain attitude or disposition toward thinking. This attitude is open, curious, and speculative, and is indifferent to conclusions and achieving any sense of self-certainty.

THEORY DOES NOT NEED YOUR PATRONAGE

With this in mind, I would like to question whether or not theory (in any of its variants) should be required as part of an architectural education. Moreover, I would like to challenge the notion that theory needs to be preserved within the academy. At its best, theory is not one with itself. If we free ourselves from the idea that theory is self-contained and is in need of saving then we can begin to liberate theory from having to justify its position in the education, training, and formation of a young designer. If that means that theory goes away or becomes something else, so be it. Theory, if it is to have any material value, must be self-sustaining, and should make no appeal to the patronage of any profession or discipline, including architecture.

WHAT DO WE MEAN WHEN WE USE THE WORD "THEORY"?

I don't know if my understanding of theory is shared by those reading this. I also suspect that my understanding of theory has changed over time and will continue to do so. I've used the word to express a range of related yet distinct activities, such as: questioning, problematizing, thinking, analyzing, imagining, relating, speculating, inquiring, determining, positioning, judging, etc. These activities, in turn, have been applied to a seemingly inexhaustible and limitless range of ideas, contexts, situations, and operations. We have aesthetic theory and game theory, quantum theory and critical theory, the special theory of relativity and attachment theory, theories of everything and theories of nothing. So, can anything be turned into a theory? What are the criteria with which to evaluate (the success, the effectiveness, the validity, the coherence, or the failure of) one theory over another? Why does theory matter?

STICKINESS

The more I think about theory, the more questions I have. What are its aims? What are its limits? Who is its audience? Can anything *be* a theory? Can anything *have* a theory? Perhaps theory's potential for adaptability and adoptability—its ability to accommodate and also be promiscuous—is one of its greatest gifts. Perhaps this virtue is also what makes theory such an intoxicating vice. Perhaps theory's pervasiveness and robustness have to do with its own theoretical vacuity, i.e. that which enables it to stretch also allows it to stick.

JUDGING

I would like to make a case for a disposition toward thinking informed by judgment. Following the political theorist Hannah Arendt, I would like to defend the double action of thinking and judging as a substitute, or possibly surrogate, for the act of theorizing and the activity of "doing theory" (whatever that means). Fundamental to thinking and judging is speaking, with oneself and with others, and questioning, that is, approaching an issue with curiosity and doubt, possibly colored by wonder or disappointment. Beginning with thinking and judging anticipates the kind of understanding that is crucial in cultivating one's ability to orient oneself in a world of constant change and human finitude, or, borrowing from Arendt (in turn borrowing from Hegel), to reconcile oneself with reality.

INVENTION

The philosopher Gilles Deleuze describes philosophy as an inventive discipline. Like film or painting, philosophy is a creative act, bringing concepts into being. Concepts, according to Deleuze, do not exist ready-made, waiting for someone to seize and deploy them at just the right time. Yes, there must be an urgency, without which there can be no creative act, but this urgency does not define its terms prior to the act of invention. Concepts must be invented; theories must also be invented. Theories are fabrications, constructs born of both truth and artifice, fictions capable of temporarily compelling reality to reframe what is possible.

OPENING

If I hesitate or am reluctant to use the word theory—especially when applied to architecture—it is because so much of what is written today in the name of theory begins with a defensive posture to the world, as if theory's greatest urgency is its self-justification. This is why I am averse to framing any discussion about architectural theory as a defense of theory as such. Demonstrative justifications tend toward compulsion, which shuts down thought rather than enabling it. In other words, justification threatens to turn a space of exchange into a space of determination and causality, moving further away from a dialogical mode of thought (which begins with the ontological fact of difference), into a monological—dare I say solipsistic—mode of compulsory agreement. Thinking-oriented-theory, which I am all for, is a relentless commitment to the present and allows us to delaminate things that have been fused by history and hardened by thoughtlessness; in other words, it enables us to unstick things that have become stuck.

Look... all I'm really saying is that I don't want to continue having the same four or five conversations with the same eight or nine people for the rest of my life. I think we need to be open, which means being open to the possibility of change, the possibility that things—including our received notions and habitual ways of thinking and doing—will be different.

ACTIVATION

For theory to be an active force in the world, capable of producing or inciting change, it cannot be passive or static, that is, given.

MAKING THINGS MATTER

Theories can be instructive in the way that diagrams can be informative. They can be deep and complex, establishing connections and relationships between thoughts and things; or they can be shallow and simple, serving as intellectual guideposts or explanatory shortcuts, suggesting a way out or through. In either case, theories generate possibilities. Theory—descriptive, analytical, diagnostic, critical, speculative, projective, operative, prescriptive, or however one qualifies it—makes things meaningful, even if only to the extent that it makes a claim on our attention by saying "this matters."

There are many reasons why we say that something matters, but I am most interested in the way this act shifts our view and orientation to the world. This change in perspective has the potential to introduce new or alternative understandings. Perhaps this is one way that theory and vision are connected, at least etymologically (the Greek *theoria* having to do with seeing): giving our attention draws us in, moves us closer.

CUTTING

> *"Theory is by definition critical, in the sense of opening up to the other. Critical theory just means not being asleep. It's not much more than that."*
> *–Mark Wigley, "Flash Theory" (2015)*

I would like to revisit the coupling *critical theory* in order to make a case for a kind of theory that is one and the same as practice, but without predicating critique upon the imperative for self-reflection. The kind of theory that I have in mind is critical not in the tradition of Hegelian dialectics (i.e. in the tradition of Hegel, Marx, and Adorno: critique as self-reflective overcoming and/or negation), but critical in the tradition of the Greek *krinein,* which means to cut, to separate, to divide, to decide, to discern, to distinguish. Critique as cut demands a decision of significant consequence, as in a medical situation where one either lives or dies based on the decisive cut of a medical professional.

> *"...knowledge is not made for understanding; it is made for cutting."*
> *–Michel Foucault, "Nietzsche, Genealogy, History" (1978)*

Incisive cutting. Decision happens in a moment of urgency. Even in its more descriptive moods, critique responds to what is given speculatively, opening to difference if only through the power of suggestion. In other words, critique is a fiction inventing the truth of its reality in real time. Whether explicitly or implicitly, critique makes claims about how things ought to be. Absent this normative impulse, critique is too dull an instrument for cutting.

Krinein is also the origin of the English *crisis.* Recalling this etymological relation reminds us that we can read critique as either a cause, a response, or both cause and response to a crisis. For example: the crisis of tradition and authority following the secularization and rationalization of social, economic, and political life in the 18th century demanded a reevaluation of the limits and scope of human knowledge through the coupling of critique and reason (see Kant). Reason, one of the hallmarks of the Enlightenment project, enabled concepts like judgment and beauty to be critiqued. Bound by reason, critique offered conceptual purification through the internal analysis of a subject without the imposition of external prejudices, beliefs, and opinions, i.e. critique on its own terms. Following the authority of one's own reason is one of the features that distinguishes critique from criticism (the latter relying on ideas external to a subject—or to a work—to attain validity).

This, the shortest of detours through what critique meant to Enlightenment philosophy, is intended to provide a foil to the kind of critique I am advocating for: thought capable of transgressing reason's internal policing of the knowable. I would rather forgo conceptual purification for conceptual invention. It's hard to be open to the other when preoccupied with oneself.

EXCHANGE

Marx's critique of ideology is a form of immanent critique in the sense that it refuses to stand outside and apart from its object, society. Throughout Marx's texts we find an equivalence between critique and practice. Critique activates philosophy, rendering it free from idealism and subjectivism, by reaching outside of the mind and engaging with the world. In other words, critique is the practice of social change. Moving from the singular "I" to the collective "We" is one of the features that distinguishes philosophy from political theory. My formal training is in political theory, and as a reader of Arendt, I am committed to affirming the freedom and equality of all beings in terms of plurality. With the "more than one" in mind, I take seriously Marx's demand: "... what we have to accomplish in the present—I am speaking of a ruthless criticism of everything existing, ruthless in two senses: the criticism must not be afraid of its own conclusions, nor of conflict with the powers that be."[1] With this declaration, Marx makes clear that critique must be directed both internally and externally. By opening itself to the outside, critique also opens itself up to the other (see Derrida). If such an opening allows for exchange, things can get messy. Porosity could give way to cross-pollination or cross-contamination. You, or at least your thinking, might change. Perhaps this is what it means to have an open mind?

If adopted and put into practice, what might a refigured notion of critique do to/with/for architecture theory? Would architecture cut parts

---

1 Karl Marx, "For a Ruthless Criticism of Everything Existing," in *The Marx-Engels Reader*, ed. Robert C. Tucker (New York: Norton, 1972), 13.

of itself off to survive the traumas of theory? Critique as self-amputation.

FORCE

"In architecture, as in several other areas of knowledge, theory and practice are so closely intertwined that any attempt to negate one term at the expense of the other means the extinction of both. Kill theory and practice dies. Kill practice and theory dies."
–Bernard Tschumi "Some Notes on Architectural Theory" (2015)

Pace Kant, critique is not a consequence of reason. Pace Marx, critique is not revealed by an analysis of the contradictions of social relations. Critique makes no truth claims for itself. It is without justification. Its only support is the force of its articulation. If critique has any power at all, it is the power of transformability.[2]

What does this mean for critical theory today? For theory and practice? Certainly, the relay between theory and practice should not be one of rule-following, nor should it be mere affirmation. As an act of design, theory will postulate, speculate, and invent new realities, making decisions that are critical in every sense of the word.

URGENCY

"Theory is the flash that allows architecture to be seen as a lingering afterimage. For a moment it's blinding, but there is an afterimage within which there is a sense of what architecture is."
–Mark Wigley, "Flash Theory" (2015)

---

2 Nietzsche's "On the Uses and Disadvantages of History for Life" is particularly instructive on this point. The essay contains a passage that cuts to the core of historicism and lays bare the conservatism of a culture evacuated of the "plastic" and transformative power of critique. "The work never produces an effect but only another 'critique'; and the critique produces no effect either, but again only a further critique. There thus arises a general agreement to regard the acquisition of many critiques as a sign of success, of few or none as a sign of failure. At bottom, however, even given this kind of 'effect' everything remains as it was: people have some new thing to chatter about for a while, and then something newer still, and in the meantime go on doing what they have always done. The historical culture of our critics will no longer permit any effect at all in the proper sense, that is an effect on life and action□." Friedrich Nietzsche, "On the Uses and Disadvantages of History for Life," (1873) in *Nietzsche: Untimely Meditations,* ed. Daniel Breazeale (Cambridge: Cambridge University Press, 1997), 87.

If, following Wigley, theory is the flash that gives visibility to architecture, what are the enabling conditions of this flash? What is its temporality, duration, structure?

Walter Benjamin's dialectical image [*dialektisches Bild*], a concept in need of illumination if there ever was one, moves us closer to answering the questions suggested by Wigley's account of *flash theory*. Dialectical images are thought-figures that manifest alternative temporalities to the sequential ordering of linear time, breaking with rule-governed processes of cognition.[3] Beginning with the latter of the two terms, *image* suggests the arrest of movement, while *dialectical* implies movement and change. The coupling *dialectical image* allows the conceptual pairing to maintain a proximity and distance that is both spatial and temporal, that is, perspective. Yet this perspective is more partial than totalizing. By virtue of its incompleteness, such perspective provides more filter than focus, more haze than clarity.[4] Benjamin's dialectical image is not a representation, but a convergence, a simultaneity of then and now. With Benjamin, the relation between past and present, and image and thought, is figural, not temporal.

Adorno characterizes this figural relation of past and present as a constellation.[5] It is worth noting that this mode of presentation is the

---

3 Dialectical images are not pictorial, but ephemeral flashings or affections of experience. Neither purely mental nor material representations, they evince a constellation of resemblances whose form and content are indistinguishable.

4 "For theory to be an agent of vision in this sense does not presuppose clarity. Theory doesn't come along and simply illuminate things. On the contrary, to see, or to see seeing, or to see architecture as that which allows you to see, is precisely to respect the blur, the murkiness, the doubling, the vibrations, the contradictions, the instabilities, the space in which an image could appear." Mark Wigley, "Flash Theory," in *2000+ The Urgencies of Architectural Theory*, ed. James Graham (New York: GSAPP Books, 2015), 275.

5 Dialectical images, writes Adorno, are "constellations of historical entities which do not remain simply interchangeable examples for ideas but which in their uniqueness constitute the ideas themselves as historical." Absent the will for totality and mastery, the term constellation draws our attention to the indeterminacy of relations, as opposed to their identification. As ephemeral configurations, constellations emerge and recede. As affective correspondences, constellations are not beholden to the rules of knowledge claims, nor do they rely upon empirical verification for their validity. While cognitive and empirical propositions validate claims to rational truth, they do not account for the appearance of that which resists identification, that is, forms of thought like constellations, which have no logical necessity. Dialectical images signify relations which are external to their terms. Theodor Adorno, "A Portrait of Walter Benjamin,"

opposite of what we find in our architecture theory readers, which disclose their historical condition less as figural convergence and more as chronologically situated presentations of architectural thought: Ulrich Conrads and Michael Bullock, *Programs and Manifestoes on 20th-Century Architecture* (1971); Kate Nesbitt, *Theorizing a New Agenda for Architecture: An Anthology of Architectural Theory 1965-1995* (1996); K. Michael Hays, *Architecture Theory since 1968* (2000); A. Krista Sykes, *Constructing a New Agenda: Architectural Theory 1993-2009* (2010); James Graham, *2000+: The Urgencies of Architectural Theory* (2015). Of these five edited volumes, Graham's title *2000+* names the requisite openness demanded of architectural theory as a condition of historical urgency. The temporal horizon of theory—critical theory, architecture theory, or any other theory, I argue—cannot be given or known in advance. Theory's urgency "is precisely that which is not yet agreed upon, and not yet seen."[6]

I find pairing Wigley's formulation of flash theory with Benjamin's dialectical image to be productive for thinking about theory now, as both describe events whose duration, extent, and effect cannot be prefigured. Between past and future (to once again borrow from Arendt), we in the present have the opportunity, should we seize it, to make an incisive cut, a critical decision, capable of seeing and building the world anew.

QUESTIONS FOR THE READER

Why read, write, and produce theory?
What is theory's relationship to history?
Who does theory speak for?
Theory as collective enterprise or theory as private activity?
Theory as operative act or interpretive lens?
Theory as grounding or destabilizing of ground?
Theory and practice? Theory as practice? Practice as theory? •

Prisms, trans. Samuel and Shierry Weber (Cambridge: MIT Press, 1998), 231–238.

6 Wigley, "Flash Theory," 268.

Generational Shifts, Criticality, and the Relevance of Architectural Theory Today

Gabriel Fuentes

> "I believe I drank too much wine last night at Hurstbourne; I know not how else to account for the shaking of my hand today. You will kindly make allowance therefore for any indistinctness of writing, by attributing it to this venial error."
> –Jane Austen

> "Thanx for ur txt last night. ended up gettin totaly maggotd n my hands r still shakin dis mornin so if any typos thats y."
> –Jane Austen via text message[1]

When considering the state of architectural theory and its pedagogies, we must ask: *who* is theory for? Who, in other words, are we teaching? What shapes *their* world? And how is architectural theory relevant for them? Today's architecture students are part of the first generation born into a hyper-integrated world—digital natives of a neoliberal eco-informational society. Coming of age in the aftermath of 9/11 and the 2008 financial crisis, their worldviews are influenced largely by the socio-economic inequalities of neoliberalism, ubiquitous technology, and the flattening effects of network culture layered onto the institutional (infra)structures set in place by their Silent and Boomer elders. As a result, they have been subject to extreme (mis) characterizations, ranging from Mark Bauerlein's characterization as the "dumbest generation" to what Neil Howe and William Struss call the "next great generation," a generation of heroes poised to bring about massive global change.[2]

In what follows, I trace collective and meta-critical shifts in architecture along the Howe-Strauss generational theory model—situating architecture's theoretical turns and historiographical pressure points (1968 being one of many) as symptoms of these broader generational shifts. Seen this way, the so-called "problem" or "death" of theory should not be misconstrued as an outright lack of criticality. To the contrary, the "post-critical" tendency to be critical *toward* theory reflects the same "post-modern" tendency to theorize modernity *against*

---

1 Mark McCrindle and Emily Wolfinger, "Influences on 21st Century Language," in *Word Up: A Lexicon and Guide to Communication in the 21st Century* (Braddon, AU: Halstead Press, 2011).

2 For more on Bauerlein's position, see: Mark Bauerlein, *The Dumbest Generation: How the Digital Age Stupefies Young Americans and Jeopardizes our Culture: Or, Don't Trust Anyone Under 30* (New York: Penguin Group, 2008).

modernism.[3] Both are symptomatic of larger generational cycles through which different generations negotiate their places in history.

In *Generations: The History of America's Future, 1584 to 2069,* Howe and Strauss claim that generations develop along four distinct phases (childhood, young adulthood, midlife, and elderhood) over a span of eighty to a hundred years.[4] With a birth span of twenty to twenty-five years in between, each generation defines their values around a constellation of historic events, pressing (or trending) issues, and contemporary technologies.[5] Having their strongest collective agency during young adulthood and midlife, each generation challenges, without always subverting, the strictures of previous generations while constructing the milieu of the next.

Over the 20th century (and into the 21st), this milieu has been defined by a constellation of seven generations: the Lost Generation (b. 1883-1901); the G.I. Generation (b. 1902-1924); the Silent Generation (b. 1925-1942); the Baby Boom (b. 1943-1960); Generation X (b. 1961-1981); Generation Y or The Millennials (b. 1982-1991); and Generation Z (b. 1992-2009).[6] As the offspring of late-Generation X/early-Generation Y, today's architecture students (Z'ers) are the first born into a technologically connected world. Yet while the information economy offers them the advantage of being the most global generation in history, it cannot be separated from dysfunctional politics, global terrorism, economic uncertainty, social inequality, overt racism and xenophobia, corporate corruption, and environmental crisis, forces that have increasingly impacted architectural theory, education, and

---

3 Postmodern discourses were (indeed are) symptomatic of Modernity's internal contradictions as it negotiated the antifoundational, and hence hegemonic, forces of late capitalism. In this sense, Modernism—as a set of early 20th century aesthetic practices—lost its political and social agency as it fell one generation behind Modernity—the socio-psychological and philosophical conditions of "being modern," or "contemporary."

4 Neil Howe and William Strauss, *Generations: The History of America's Future, 1584 to 2069* (New York: William Morrow and Company, 1991).

5 Technology and media, whether television and radio in the 20th century or social media platforms and artificial intelligence in the 21st, play a significant aesthetic and political role in mediating social values and systems of meaning across generations.

6 That this model is limited *to* and *by* a clear Anglo-American framework demonstrates both the opportunity and the critical need to widen the frame to include non-Western contexts—or, perhaps better said, to displace the West (particularly North America and the United Kingdom) from the evolutionary center of global culture.

practice in the 21st century.

Little wonder that theory has died a thousand deaths. To discourse on these issues can almost seem unethical, an intellectual indulgence that enables us to spin our linguistic wheels self-servingly while the world spins to ecological destruction, or a naive academic pursuit that distances us from the very markets that empower our capacity to initiate innovation and change (capitalism, after all, thrives on crisis). In "After Theory," Michael Speaks draws a generational line through the sand of architectural discourse by attacking architectural education's failure to "recognize the fundamental nature of the challenges confronting architecture in a world increasingly dominated by technological change and marketization," insisting that while schools have adequately instilled digital competency, they have "largely failed to develop an intellectual culture that would enable students to make the best use of these skills in a marketplace that puts such a high value on innovation."[7] Theory, he claims, handicaps innovation by advancing Enlightenment ideals of ultimate truth and by splitting thinking from doing; that is, by asserting that "manifestos *guide* political action; that architectural theory *guides* architectural practice."[8] In a post-theoretical world, architectural theory must give way to a strategic and pragmatic realism capable of engaging our market-driven world rather than resisting it via anachronistic models of thinking (e.g. Deconstruction or Marxism). Architecture must operate, as Stan Allen writes, "*in* and *on* the world," not as commentary *about* the world.

But Speaks's argument for "post-theoretical" practices is neither anti-theoretical nor "post-critical" (a term applied to him by George Baird that he, in any case, denies).[9] To be sure, he resists, negates, and offers alternatives to the modes of architectural thinking and practice promoted by K. Michael Hays and Peter Eisenman. In other words, he is not *acritical* but rather *critical of a particular kind of criticality*.[10] In his *theory of atheoretical practice,* architecture engages the world affirmatively by *resisting resistance* (*Oppositions,* anyone?).

To resist resistance is to be both frustrated by and optimistic about the status quo—a middle-ground position that resonates with a generation overwhelmed by ever-changing news cycles (or media streams) that flicker between hope and doom. In *Millennials Rising,* Howe

---

7 Michael Speaks, "After Theory," *Architectural Record* 193, no. 6 (June 2005).

8 Ibid.

9 George Baird, "Criticality and Its Discontents," *Harvard Design Magazine* 21 (Fall 2004/Winter 2005).

10 It should be noted that Speaks never used the term "post-critical."

and Strauss predicted that the Millennial Generation (according to some, a generational constellation of Generation Y and Generation Z)[11] would be heroes and rebuilders during the next crisis age, which they have since pegged to the economic recession of 2008.[12] More numerous, affluent, educated, and diverse than previous generations, this generation, they argued, would recast the Boomers' narcissistic emphasis on talk over action and Generation X's youthful image of free agency and alienation, emphasizing collaboration, modesty, kindness, good conduct, ethics, and social justice. They based their prediction on a close study of Anglo-American history that reveals cyclical patterns and generational archetypes.[13] If history is influenced by generations and vice versa, they argue, the two form a symbiosis between time and life. And if one is seasonal, the other must be also.

In an earlier book, *The Fourth Turning,* Howe and Strauss argue that history oscillates on a pendulum in response to generational patterns and conflicts.[14] The structure that binds these historical rhythms is the *saeculum,* an ancient Roman term used to define a long human life or a natural century.[15] Within each *saeculum,* they argue, societies turn at least

---

11 There is some discrepancy in the way generational theorists define the beginning and end of generations. While Howe and Strauss mark the Millennial Generation as born between 1982-2004, followed by the Homeland Generation born in 2005 and beyond (they do not recognize a Generation Z), Australian researcher Mark McCrindle argues that the speed of social, political, and economic change enabled by technology has triggered the emergence of a new generation born after 1991 (what he calls Gen Z). Hence what Howe and Strauss consider one Millennial Generation, McCrindle considers two, Gen Y (1982-1991) and Gen Z (1992-2009), respectively. McCrindle calls the next generation (2010-?) Generation Alpha.

12 Neil Howe and William Strauss, *Millennials Rising: The Next Great Generation* (New York: Vintage Books, 2000).

13 While the arguments of this chapter are filtered through and limited in scope by an Anglo-American framework, it is important to note that as a historical-theoretical model, Generational Theory is, or at least should be, applicable across many cultural and geographic contexts. I hope that this chapter opens up the critical need to expand Howe and Strauss' work toward non-Western contexts and provides a foundation for further research.

14 Neil Howe and William Strauss, *The Fourth Turning: An American Prophecy—What the Cycles of History Tell Us About America's Next Rendezvous with Destiny* (New York: Broadway Books, 1997).

15 According to Howe and Strauss, Anglo-American history has gone through six full *seacula* and is currently on its seventh: 1. Late Medieval Period (?-1486), 2. Reformation Period (1487-1593), 3. New World Period (1594-1703), 4. Revolutionary Period (1704-1793), 5. Civil War Period

four times in line with the life-phase shifts of current generations and the birth of new ones, roughly every twenty to twenty-five years. Each generational "turning" is akin to a climactic season in a four-season cycle with two extreme periods (summer and winter) and two mild ones (spring and fall). And because we can rely on the certainty of seasons, and yet no two seasons are exactly alike, history always resets itself structurally without ever repeating itself specifically.

Along this model (its teleology notwithstanding), every generational turn brings predictable changes in collective moods and dispositions as generational constellations re-shift and current generations compensate for the perceived excesses of older ones. First turnings (mild springs) are *High* periods, times when new civic structures replace old values, collectivism is strong, and individualism is weak; second turnings (extreme summers) are *Awakening* periods, times when youth are volatile and critical of the civic and institutional structures of previous generations; third turnings (mild falls) are *Unraveling* periods, times when civic and institutional structures are at their weakest and individualism peaks; and fourth turnings (extreme winter) are *Crisis* periods, times of major social change, collective restructuring, and civic/institutional rebuilding. In this model, Generation Z is a hero generation coming of age during the fourth turning of the Millennial *Saeculum*, the lineage of which began in the US with the postwar American High (first turning, 1946-1964), transitioned to the Consciousness Revolution of the late 1960s and the culture wars of the '80s, '90s, and early 2000s (second and third turnings, respectively), before transitioning to our current global crisis period (2008-2029?), driven by neoliberal capitalism and climate change.[16]

Architectural theory, of course, turns along with these generational shifts, which often form the foundation of what is recorded as history. During the Consciousness Revolution of the long '70s, for example, architectural theory was driven by a *crisis of meaning* which was interrogated by early postmodernist practices that were dialectical, negational, introverted, and narrowly focused on disciplinary autonomy. Theory was the weapon of a young, aggressive, and reflective generation grappling with the failures (real or perceived) of their forefathers: the unfulfilled promises of heroic Modernism. It was indeed

---

(1794-1864), 6. Great Power Period (1865-1945), and 7. Millennial Period (1946-2029?).

16 For an in-depth study of generational history, theory, and dynamics, refer to Neil Howe's Life Course Associates Website, www.lifecourse.com/.

an *Awakening;* such critical practices reflected a disillusioned postwar youth that questioned everything from the very need for architecture to the cultural, institutional, and political structures put in place by previous generations. The so-called death of Modernism (symbolized by the televised demolition of the Pruitt-Igoe Housing complex in 1972) along with the intensifying Cold War, the John F. Kennedy and Martin Luther King Jr. assassinations, the war in Vietnam, the 1968 riots, Woodstock, Watergate, and the oil crisis, gave rise to a range of counter-cultural movements aimed at disrupting the status quo.

Individualism and disruption leads to *Unraveling.* The third turning of architectural theory—driven by weak collectivity and developing during the culture wars of the 1980s and 1990s—celebrated discourse and difference around Foucault, Deleuze, and Derrida (and also Venturi, Tafuri, and Rossi). The Reagan and Thatcher years of rising neoliberalism, strengthening consumer culture, and the dot-com boom combined with the LA riots, widening inequality and racism, and MTV, gave rise to gangster rap, grunge, mallrats, and a new wave of critical theory. But because late postmodernism's anti-foundational project reduced the social to a system of differences divorced from the ideologies and institutions set in place by modernity, its criticality failed to foster collective agency for long-term institutional change. Witness the *crisis of theory* (and not necessarily *meaning*) and the rise of "post-criticality" in architecture into the 21st century.

But whither criticality? With Silicon Valley startups perfecting deepfake technology and the sixteen-year-old climate activist Greta Thunberg named Time's 2019 "Person of the Year," can we really claim that today's youth passively accept the status quo? Whereas Boomers and Gen X'ers—characterized by their parochial self-reflection—used theory to disrupt neoliberalism (without any real hope of overcoming it), Gen Z is intellectually agile and forward-looking; rather than withdrawing into autonomy, they seek immediate material consequences for their actions. They are practice-driven; with (a capacity for) derivative intelligence, they are less interested in moral and philosophical complexity, authenticity, and "original" culture. Hence, if theory was once used as a weapon to resist, escape, or destroy the system, today's generation has a different arsenal for a different mission: armed with technology, algorithms, and a networked collective force, they are geared to hack into the system, to expand and reshape it from within to be more just, equitable, and inclusive. Instead of resisting capitalism through sophisticated theoretical procedures, they work reflexively *within*

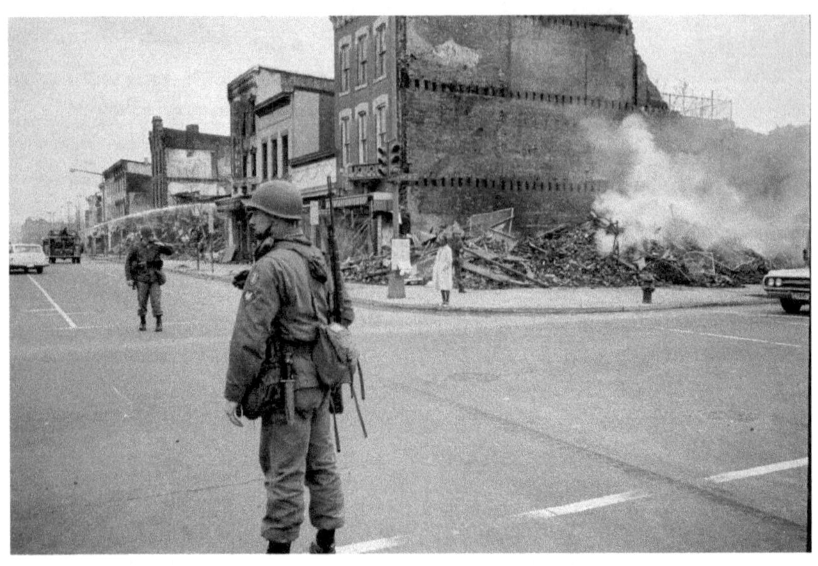

F I G 1 :
A soldier stands on the corner of 7th & N Street NW in Washington D.C. in front of buildings that were destroyed during the riots following the assassination of Martin Luther King, Jr., April 8th, 1968.

Photo: Warren K. Leffler https://en.wikipedia.org/wiki/Kingassassination_riots#/media File:Leffler_-_968Washington,_D.C._Martin_Luther_King,_Jr._riots.jpg

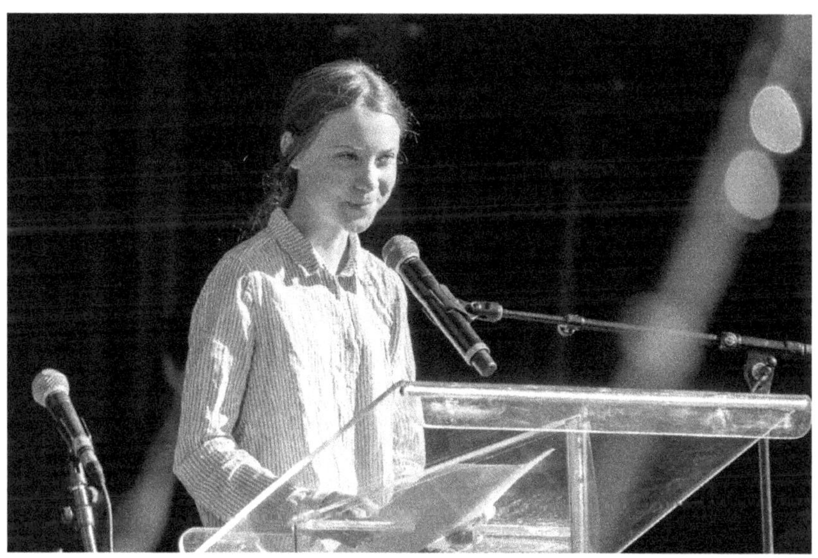

FIG 2:
Sixteen-year-old Greta Thunberg speaking at a Climate March in Montreal, Canada, September 27th, 2019.

Photo: Lëa-Kim Châteauneuf https://en.wikipedia.org/wiki/Greta_Thunberg#/media/File:Marche_pour_le_climat_27-09-2019_(Montr%C3%A9al)_14.jpg and *against* it (or, put differently, they work within capitalism *in order to* work against it, against capitalism *in order to* work within it), seeking opportunities to carve niches within society itself. Wittingly or not, they are critical but not necessarily negational.

So where does this leave theory when Gen Z students seem so indifferent to big ideas, when immediate gratification trumps the hard work of critical discourse? Students starting out today were affected by 9/11 and Bush's Global War on Terror, the 2008 economic crisis, and, most recently, the polarizing cultural and political landscape triggered by Brexit and the Trump presidency. With the world in such turmoil, who has time to indulge in slow, big picture, structurally critical, and self-reflective theory? Isn't the world too complex to understand, too entwined to disentangle? Doesn't theory—distant and abstract—preclude action? What good does it do when confined to the white walls of the academy?

In fact, it still does a lot. Theory has the benefit of being both historically situated and critically distanced, institutionally backed but not market-driven. Because of this, theory enables architecture to operate from the middle-in; that is, to engage the world from a uniquely disciplinary position, one that considers the specifically architectural (form, space, aesthetics, materials, systems, etc.) with the same intensity as it does the structural conditions that frame and enable it (the social, cultural, political, economic, and environmental contexts). Theory, in other words, can open up the world *to* and *for* architecture, making it visible to and *for* a generation empowered to effect change by means other than thought models and literary revolutions. Theory itself, then, is not dead; its modes of criticality, communication, and visibility are simply subsumed in a vast social media complex that shapes, partitions, and distributes the ecologies of knowledge that in turn shape the way we define, see, and effect "the global." These modes are key to understanding the role global issues might play in contemporary theory and its pedagogies.

To make theory relevant today, we must acknowledge that Gen Z is a *platform generation* through and through—their systems of meaning are in constant flux precisely because they are both grounded pragmatically in the world (socially, physically, economically) and digitally mediated. As Mark Wigley pointed out during a debate with Peter Eisenman regarding the status of "ground" in architecture, "this generation is grounded in the digital," not, as Eisenman would have it, in the metaphysics of presence. He continues,

> "...the concept of 'ground' has moved into the digital... (hence) it is more true to say that a building today stands (more) on the digital platforms with which it was conceived than on the (actual) site. Or to restate that same point, digital platforms ARE THE SITE; buildings are literally constructed in the space of digital transactions, a version of which could be dropped onto what we used to call a (physical) site..."[17]

In a media-saturated world, information platforms condition the relational and representational dimensions of architectural theory, its sites, and its pedagogies. The surface is the medium and the medium is the message. But who is the message for? What kind of message is architecture willing to engage?

According to Marc Prensky, social media is not as remarkable in itself as in its capacity to *enable* (now, reread the sentence with "theory" in place of "social media"). In other words, the inherent programmability of social media lends us the ability to channel mass anxiety toward collective action (or, perhaps, *re*action). In "The Death of Command and Control?" he argues that, through social media, today's generation can shift our core concepts of democracy from within as their collective agency grows and strengthens.[18] Hacking the systems once deemed closed —from corporations and politics to education, pop culture, and indeed architectural practice—they are (re)designing and supporting the software that enables institutional change. But we must distinguish *criticality* as reactive angst from *critique* as systematic analysis. As the youth climate protests, #MeToo movement, Black Lives Matter, and the Parkland shooting protests (to name a few) have all recently shown, criticality is alive and well among today's youth. But many are effecting (or *wanting* to effect) immediate change without structural critique—the potential agency of critical theory has been replaced by what Nick Srnicek and Alex Williams call *folk politics.*

In *Inventing the Future: Postcapitalism and a World Without Work,* Srnicek and Williams describe folk politics as a "collective and historically

---

17 Mark Wigley, "Wobble: The Cat Has Nine Lives," debate with Peter Eisenman at Columbia University, Graduate School of Architecture, Planning and Preservation on September 12, 2012, www.youtube.com/watch?v=Gu4-ErX6hDA.

18 Marc Prensky, "The Death of Command and Control?" in *Technology Alliance Partners,* January 20th, 2004, accessed February 18, 2013, www.marcprensky.com/writing/prensky-sns-01-20-04.pdf.

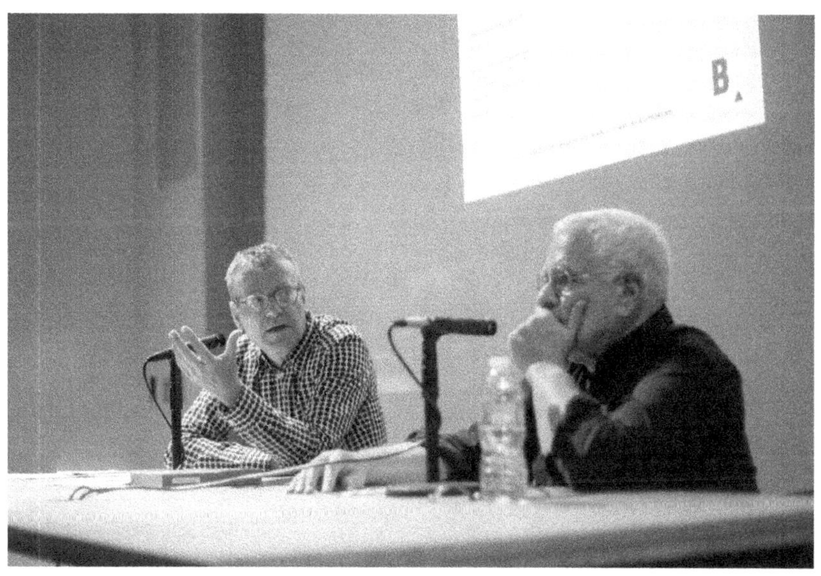

FIG 3:
Mark Wigley and Peter Eisenman discuss the status of "ground" in architecture during a public debate at Columbia University's Graduate School of Architecture, Planning and Preservation on September 12th, 2012.
Photo: https://www.flickr.com/photos/gsapponline/7983645335/

constructed political common sense that has become out of joint with the actual mechanisms of power."[19] In other words, by scaling global problems down to human scale, folk politics operate locally on the surface—reducing the overwhelming structural complexity of our neoliberal world to something affective, tangible, and thinkable by emphasizing temporal, spatial, and conceptual immediacy over large-scale, long-term strategy (all that is relevant evaporates into media). If critical architectural theory was at one point radical in its structural critique, the social relevance and political agency of such critique is now muted within the ubiquitous white noise of a fragmented collective hegemonically conditioned by finance capitalism and its infrastructures. There is no outside: if architecture is to resist anything, it can only do so incrementally from within the system[20]—Manfredo Tafuri meets Post Malone.

But while architectural practice—in its focus on the building scale, the local and affective, the collaborative and participatory, the material and its processes of construction—might be considered a folk political practice (or, at least, a practice conditioned by a kind of folk political thinking that maintains a gap between architecture's desire for deep structural change and its actual ability to effect it), architectural theory has the capacity to resist from within by reorienting and reconfiguring the infrastructures that condition both architectural and public discourse. Its strongest critical agency lies in its ability to collapse the scale(s) at which architecture operates, pulling the local and the global into each other as it (re)draws history in its own image.[21] For Gen Z, then, theory is a platform for hacking the world *through* practice, and vice versa.

Of course, time will tell if and how Generation Z—the hero generation of the Millennial *Saeculum*—will bring about the large-scale, long-term structural changes predicted by Howe and Struss. But one thing holds true: even though today's architecture students (and future architects/theorists) do not recognize—indeed, are conditioned never

---

19 Nick Srnicek and Alex Williams, *Inventing the Future: Postcapitalism and a World Without Work* (London: Verso, 2016).

20 See: David Harvey, *The Condition of Postmodernity: An Enquiry into the Origins of Cultural Change* (Malden, MA: Blackwell Publishers, 1990).

21 In this sense, architectural theory not only remains true to its historical meaning as both critical contemplation (*theoria, theoros*) and theater (*thea*), but it also, and inescapably, risks (for better or worse) operating as what Srnicek and Williams describe as a "folk-political injunction...to reduce complexity down to human scale."

to imagine—a world outside of the oppressive hegemonic forces of neoliberal capitalism, their experiences within the system have not dulled their sense of angst, their desire for change, nor their disposition for action. If theory is in crisis, it is not for lack of criticality; what traditional architectural theory lacks, indeed what it has always lacked, is the ability to *exercise* the power necessary to transform capitalism.[22] Hence the relevance of architectural theory today—in an interconnected yet fragmented, eco-informational society—is not its traditional role as an instigator and protector of grand metanarratives, but rather its *representational* and *infrastructural* capacity to infuse the system and turn it against itself... at least until the next spring. •

---

22 In this area, the Right has overwhelmed and outmaneuvered the Left, by now all but subsumed under the hegemonic forces of neoliberalism. While effective as modes of disruption, traditional leftist tactics (analyzing, protesting, unionizing, striking, occupying, theorizing, etc.) often fall short of strategically engaging the deep structural conditions necessary for political change (evidenced by our current state of socio-economic inequalities and environmental crisis). As an aesthetic and political practice – and theorizing is indeed a kind of practice – architecture's critical capacity lies largely in its ability to fuse the radical tactics of the Left with the hegemonic strategies of the Right around strong ethical values, hybridizing new modes of theory and design toward reconfiguring what Keller Easterling calls contemporary "matrix space."

Against a Theory of Walls: On Architectural Criticism and Decolonization

Elisa Dainese

In the last turbulent twenty years, accrediting boards, universities and schools of architecture have recognized the need for painful self-reflection on the state of the architecture discipline. As a result, the architectural curriculum has changed, foregrounding concepts such as inclusion and diversity.[1] Every day, multidisciplinary collaborations blossom and connect academic and research institutions interested in developing a multi-perspectival understanding of architecture.[2] Groups of architectural scholars produce teaching materials on the history of non-Western subjects and share them with colleagues around the world, while global architectural history survey courses flourish within architectural programs.[3] Every year schools open new positions searching for teaching experts in global topics, and departments conceive new professional roles to expose architectural students to "other" and "multiple" traditions at a rate that has no precedent in our pedagogical history.

If the architectural curriculum has opened its boundaries and reoriented its discourse, one might ask: What has happened to the theory and criticism course? Does it offer a broader and more inclusive investigation of the world of architectural ideas? Or is it still barricaded behind its disciplinary walls? The answer is not very reassuring. Despite visible efforts, theory is still often taught as a homogenous and Western-centric exercise whose rhetoric perpetuates ideas of clarity, efficiency, and cohesiveness. No matter how much more comprehensive and multidisciplinary material is produced every year, the feeling is that the

---

1 The National Architectural Accrediting Board developed its current procedures for accreditation in 2015. See NAAB, "Procedures for Accreditation" (May 6, 2015), https://www.naab.org/wp-content/uploads/2015-Procedures-Final-Approved-Edition_copyedited-052915.pdf, accessed March 7, 2020. New conditions for accreditation of architectural schools include the support of "equity, diversity and inclusion in architecture education and the profession." See NAAB, 2020 Conditions for Accreditation, Pre-Forum Review – "Draft 0" (May 20, 2019), 2, https://naab.app.box.com/v/draft0-Conditions, accessed January 10, 2020.

2 The Canadian Social Sciences and Humanities Research Council (SSHRC), for example, promotes and supports research in architecture, the humanities, and social sciences by focusing on forging connections across campuses and communities, https://www.canada.ca/en/social-sciences-humanities-research.html, accessed March 9, 2020.

3 See, for example, the initiatives developed by the Global Architectural History Teaching Collaborative (GAHTC) by Mark Jarzombek and Vikramaditya Prakash, http://gahtc.org, and the Aggregate Architectural History Collaborative (AAHC), http://we-aggregate.org.

architectural research on diversity and the global explorations in architectural history are just beginning, while theory and criticism are not even able to catch up with this discourse on global knowledge.

The ability to adapt to change is a foundational characteristic of the theoretical project. The pedagogy of the course on history, theory, and criticism developed in the late 1960s, when the influences of the cultural transformations and political unrest occurring in so-called Third World anticolonial struggles emerged in Western academia.[4] The roots of this project were deep in that contemporary mixture of civil and anti-colonial rights movements, student and social struggles, anti-war and anti-nuclear campaigns, feminist uprisings, and gay rights activism.[5] In its transnational and subversive nature, the theoretical project helped students to connect architectural ideas with a broader understanding of the world, enjoying unparalleled success from the 1970s to the 1990s, after which, however, it almost entirely lost its allure—some scholars even declared its death, while others termed it the "theoretical meltdown."[6]

Today, in the wake of the Black Lives Matter movement and global Women's Strikes, alongside the reinvigoration of far-right groups, the refugee crisis, and environmental disasters, educators and students have become impatient to investigate these problems and pressures; they seek a way to understand them as an interconnected reality. If conditions outside the discipline have changed, by definition cultural and theoretical ideas should be able to change along with the world they reflect upon. After all, the course on history and theory was born in the postwar period, when the whole sensibility of society had undergone a fundamental transformation. With 9/11 and the War on Terror, after having come up to the brink of economic disaster, global society is experiencing another moment of profound metamorphosis. It is the shift from the postwar epoch of economic boom and excitement for the present to the paranoid and protectionist era of fierce nationalisms and spreading pandemics, concerns for the future, and global climate change. As a result, once again the humanities show signs of losing their

4 For more on this topic see Terry Eagleton, *After Theory* (London: Allen Lane, 2003).

5 See the work done by anticolonial thinkers such as Franz Fanon, or thinkers like Herbert Marcuse, Wilhelm Reich, Simone de Beauvoir, Antonio Gramsci, Theodor Adorno, Fredric Jameson, and Jean-Luc Godard.

6 Luigi Puglisi, *Architectural Design* 79, no. 1 (2009): 96–97. This special issue was entitled "Theoretical Meltdown."

innocence, while the pedagogical project of theory pauses and reflects on its own purpose and assumptions.

After the political upheavals of the last bitter years, theorists have started to think more critically about the structure of their theoretical formations, focusing on the multiple ways in which one can understand architecture's relationship to the world. Following new proposed criteria for accreditation that require architecture programs to prepare students on the "theories of architecture and urbanism, framed by broad social, cultural, economic, and political forces," critics meet to discuss the fate of architectural theory and organize conferences to talk about the discipline and where it is headed.[7] Some theorists have also developed new pedagogical projects that challenge the unstated complicity between the architectural discipline, the disciplinary structure of its theoretical formations, and the anxiety feeding contemporary practices.[8] Indeed, in the last decades, criticism has fought a society of spectacle, set "against a culture programmatically directed toward the future," and the world of production, seeking only answers to mitigate the contemporary, cognitive concerns of the architectural discipline.[9] Theory has only incompletely been able to counter the oversimplification of content sellers and information-makers, who offer a stream of palatable but trite solutions to practitioners and educators. Architecture students, especially, are increasingly susceptible to this. However

---

7 On the resurgence of theoretical investigations in the new criteria for accreditation see NAAB, Conditions for Accreditation, "Draft 1" (Sept 9, 2019), https://files.constantcontact.com/330af1cb001/34b86713-711f-493a-ade4-f8d5b01ec1c3.pdf, accessed March 7, 2020. On recent discussions on theory see, for example, the "Theory's Curriculum AA Roundtable" held by Joseph Bedford in London, UK, in May 2019, https://architecture.exchange/tc-event/aa-roundtable/; the conference "Architectural Theory Now?" organized by Franca Trubiano, David Leatherbarrow, and Peter Laurence in Philadelphia, USA, in April 2019, https://www.design.upenn.edu/architecture/graduate/events/architectural-theory-now-0; and the conference "Theory's History, 196x-199x" held by Hilde Heynen and KU Leuven/Ugent in Leuven, Belgium, in February 2017, https://architectuur.kuleuven.be/theoryshistory/.

8 On this topic see, for example, the "Theory's Curriculum Italy Workshop" held by Joseph Bedford and Joseph Godlewski in Vicenza, Italy, in May 2018. Some materials and syllabi developed during that meeting are presented in the online platform "Architecture Exchange" created to share ideas on architectural theory and pedagogies, https://architecture.exchange/curriculum/.

9 Joan Ockman, "Slashed," *e-flux architecture*, October 27, 2017, https://www.e-flux.com/architecture/history-theory/159236/slashed/.

motivated they may be to immerse themselves in their own expression and the work of others, they are trapped by the deep anxiety of a discipline that never sleeps.

When asked to explain the role of the course on history, theory, and criticism, students are confused. Theory seems an unproductive and complicated discipline, offering them little help to recover from their architectural anxiety. Borrowing from Tafuri, I tell students how history, theory, and criticism can go beyond the "symptoms of malaise" that define architecture.[10] The goal is to be immersed in the *res aedificatoria,* in what architecture says about itself, and listen to what the architectural language cannot express. Thinking (and rethinking) could help students and architects to "tear away the obfuscating veil that has been placed over the [architectural] theme by idle talk."[11]

To uncover empty and frivolous discourses, theory and criticism has recently focused on renewing the understanding of contemporary cultural developments and the world we live in. An increasing number of scholars have connected contemporary architecture, art, and media with questions of geopolitical and environmental transformation, while several other critics have articulated alternative genealogies of theoretical and political engagement investigating the institutions, social movements, and discourses that have shaped and defined architecture.[12] These theorists recognize that only new perspectives can breach the walls that traditionally protected architectural epistemologies and theories of knowledge. Only fresh attitudes can destroy the barriers erected between different disciplines and specializations. First results include publications and exhibitions that highlight how the theory of the built environment has never been straightforward or strictly disciplinary, as architects are engaged with everything that escapes rationality: war, crisis, scarcity, violence, sexuality, fetishism, disease, psychology,

---

10 Manfredo Tafuri, *History of Italian Architecture, 1944-1985* (Cambridge, Mass.: MIT Press, 1989), viii.

11 Ibid.

12 The list of scholarly materials produced by these scholars is extensive. See, for example, the alternative genealogy of the postmodern turn in American architecture developed by Felicity Scott in *Architecture or Techno-utopia: Politics after Modernism* (Cambridge, MA; MIT Press, 2010). On North American architecture education see Joan Ockman and Rebecca Williamson, *Architecture School: Three Centuries of Educating Architects in North America* (Cambridge, MA: MIT Press, 2012). See also the research on spatial practices and discourses of power and resistance produced by Ana María León as in, for example, "Prisoners of Ritoque: The Open City and the Ritoque Concentration Camp," *Journal of Architectural Education* 66, no.1 (2012) 84–97.

artificial intelligence, spontaneity, and climate change, to name a few.[13]

Scholars working on multidisciplinary topics and investigating different perspectives have questioned the limits of a theory of architecture focused on the Western canon, with only the generic inclusion of previously unstudied or "excluded" territories.[14] Their work investigates knowledge exchanges and transnational connections and challenges traditional narratives to write alternative genealogies of architecture and art.[15] Some of these theorists address established narratives of modernism and the silence on indigeneity; others investigate the contemporary overlapping of power relations, material inequalities, and social struggles, and the superficial absorption of minor voices and names.[16] Pushing this research even further, if a homogenous theory is no longer acceptable, why should Western capitalist modes of being in the world be the model against which architectural theory is measured in the course on history, theory, and criticism? After all, theory should be able to discuss the past and current

---

13 On sexuality as crisis see, for example, the work done by Beatriz Colomina on war, sexuality, and media: *Privacy and Publicity: Modern Architecture as Mass Media* (Cambridge, MA: MIT Press, 1994), and *Domesticity at War* (Cambridge, MA: MIT Press, 2007). On the constitution of contemporary subjectivity and the crisis of modernity see Rosi Braidotti, *Nomadic Subjects: Embodiment and Sexual Difference in Contemporary Feminist Theory* (New York: Columbia University Press, 1994).

14 See for example, the work developed by the Feminist Art and Architecture Collaborative (FAAC), an "intersectional feminist research group that labors in the production of new pedagogies for art and architecture" co-founded by Martina Tanga, Tessa Paneth-Pollak, Ana María León, and Olga Touloumi, https://faacweb.wordpress.com, accessed January 13, 2020. See also Feminist Art and Architecture Collaborative, "Counterplanning from the Classroom," *Journal of the Society of Architectural Historians* 76, no. 3 (September 2017): 277–280.

15 See, for example, Anooradha Iyer Siddiqi, "Architecture Culture, Humanitarian Expertise: From the Tropics to Shelter, 1953–93," *Journal of the Society of Architectural Historians* 76, no. 3 (2017): 367–84; Ginger Nolan, "Quasi-urban Citizenship: The Global Village as 'Nomos of the Modern'," *The Journal of Architecture* 23, no. 3 (2018): 448–70; and Elisa Dainese, "From the Charter of Athens to the 'Habitat': CIAM 9 and the African Grids," *The Journal of Architecture* 24, no. 3 (2019): 301–24. On the work challenging modernist paradigms in art see Elizabeth Harney and Ruth B. Phillips, *Mapping Modernisms: Art, Indigeneity, Colonialism* (Durham, NC: Duke University Press, 2018).

16 See, for example, Ana María León, "Space of Co-liberation," in *Dimensions of Citizenship,* ed. Nick Axel (Los Angeles, CA: Inventory Press LLC, 2018): 68–79; and Elisa Dainese, "The Relocation of the Indigenous Community of South Indian Lake (1966-68): For an Alternative and Shared Inhabitation of Modern Architectural History," *Thresholds* 48 (2020): 86–101.

state of the field while simultaneously reconsidering our position in it.

A change in how the architectural mind operates is necessary. The problem with several recent attempts is less a lack of criticality or geographic range than the absence of genuine exposure and receptivity. Considerable distance, for example, still exists between bodies of knowledge and the minds who investigate them. Epistemological divides still impede the reciprocity that is necessary to regain the connection between the known and the knower (including architects, educators, students, and communities). Surely, thinkers need to work to free their curricula and teaching methodologies, to "decolonize" their theoretical libraries and archives, as several scholars advocate for.[17] However, the issue does not center on redistributing knowledge and democratizing access. Only critically conscious minds and perspectives can solve such deeply rooted problems.

Through the relentless activity of thinking and rethinking, theorists should be able to challenge ideas, principles, and approaches. As guardians and patrons of the "realm of architectural ideas," for too long thinkers have lived at "the razor's edge between detachment and participation."[18] Not advocates or outcasts, they have silently witnessed the endless conflict between thinking and doing. Confronting history and theories, however, theory should be able to reveal and penetrate different perspectives, which is the way for criticism to become useful for architecture (and maybe life). In this quest, a heavy ideological burden is carried by the theoretical discipline, especially when it is interpreted as a conduit for political ideas on the workings of homogenization and globalization.[19] Theory itself becomes a condition for reasserting the relationship between agency, power, and struggle, while pedagogical research—engaged in decentering authority, disrupting disciplinary boundaries, and challenging discursive and institutional horizons—transforms into political activism.

Following this reasoning, the renovation of the course on architectural history, theory, and criticism can only start when we ethically engage with questions of participation, intersectionality, and

---

17 On the decolonization of minds, methods, and archives see, for example: NgugiWa Thiong□o. *Decolonising the Mind: The Politics of Language in African Literature* (London: Heinemann, 1986).

18 On this topic see Manfredo Tafuri, "The Historical Project," *Oppositions* 17 (1989): 65.

19 On the relation between globalization and theory see, for example, Peggy Deamer, "Globalization and the Fate of Theory," in *Global Perspectives on Critical Architecture: Praxis Reloaded*, ed. Gevork Hartoonian (Farnham, UK: Ashgate, 2015), 27–41.

empowerment in the production of knowledge—an operation that requires both an understanding of knowledge as collective inquiry and an understanding of architecture as a form of open collaboration and communal achievement.[20] It is not a coincidence that while investigating the idea of "engaged pedagogies" Hooks remembers how teaching responsible thinking is "more demanding than conventional critical or feminist pedagogy."[21] Holistic education requires the teacher to actively commit to a process of self-actualization in order to promote students' empowerment.

It is a theoretical project as much as a pedagogical one. As the Italian philosopher Giorgio Agamben explains in his book *The Coming Community*, the collective paradigm exists only in the conceptual, cultural, and physical places where communities and societies flourish or resist.[22] The role of the course on architectural history, theory, and criticism is to reveal the richness and eccentricity of the field and the hybrid nature of the discipline by exploring case studies of mainstream design groups alongside more contested figures and less-known movements and communities. The project includes challenging the idea of a hierarchical delivery of expertise, often supported by the backing of the state and its top-down deployment of governmental policies, and it translates, for example, into a profound critique of the concept of the "genius architect," still stubbornly persistent despite being openly attacked by postcolonial critics.

If the course on architectural history, theory, and criticism wants to engage in this paradigm, theory needs to re-write itself, inviting new actors in the process. Criticism's ability to challenge itself depends on greater participation in the design of courses and curricular programs by both scholars, students, and communities.[23] Indeed, "decolonize the

---

20 On the notion of open architecture and the idea of intertwined histories and theories see, for example: Esra Akcan, *Open Architecture: Migration, Citizenship, and the Urban Renewal of Berlin-Kreuzberg by IBA-1984/87* (Basel, Switzerland: Birkhauser, 2018). On architectural productive efforts beyond individualism see also George Barnett Johnston, *Drafting Culture: A Social History of Architectural Graphic Standards* (Cambridge, Mass.: MIT Press, 2008).

21 Bell Hooks, *Teaching to Transgress: Education as the Practice of Freedom* (New York: Routledge, 1994), 15.

22 Giorgio Agamben, *The Coming Community* (Minneapolis, MN: University of Minnesota Press, 1993).

23 See, for example, the pedagogical experiments conducted at Cornell by the group Critically Now: A Pop-Up and Growing Event Series, https://aap.cornell.edu/news-events/critically-now-event-series-supports-screenings-classes-exhibitions, accessed on January 10, 2020.

academy" movements, such as the South African protest movements Rhodes Must Fall and Open Stellenbosch—as well as the Rhodes Must Fall Movement in Oxford, and the Royall Must Fall Movement at Harvard—are student-driven rather than guided by educators.[24] An effective response to their call requires reforming entire institutions, curricula, and disciplines; most importantly it requires change at an individual and personal level. Fighting economic exclusion, racism, and the dehumanization of minorities, the vernacularization and Disneyfication of reality, mind colonization and cognitive imperialism, these and similar movements should help theorists to reflect on the origin of their epistemologies.[25]

As Fanon explains, decolonization is "a program of complete disorder" fighting back the violence of the colonizer.[26] The easy endorsement of decolonizing discourse by educational advocacy and scholarship, no matter how well-intended, risks producing devastating results. The academic appropriation of decolonization could backfire and defeat its very intentions—that is, the recognition of Indigenous land and cultural claims—turning decolonization into its own metaphor.[27] Conversely, I argue here that new possibilities could

---

24 The South African Rhodes Must Fall was a collective movement of students originally directed against a statue commemorating the colonial icon Cecil John Rhodes at the University of Cape Town. The campaign marked the beginning of the largest wave of student protests in democratic South Africa. Across the country, students called for the "decolonization" of universities and free higher education. For more on this topic and pedagogical transformations see Lesley Naa Norle Lokko, "The Age of Wildfire," *e-flux architectures of education,* March 20, 2020, https://www.e-flux.com/architecture/education/322674/the-age-of-wildfire/. See also Sandy Ndelu, Simamkele Dlakavu, Barbara Boswell, "Womxn's and Nonbinary Activists' Contribution to the RhodesMustFall and FeesMustFall Student Movements: 2015 and 2016," *Agenda* 31, no.3–4 (2017): 1–4.

25 For research on the decolonization of Canadian postsecondary education and its limited accessibility to Indigenous people see Battiste Marie, Lynne Bell, and L. M. Findlay, "Decolonizing Education in Canadian Universities: An Interdisciplinary, International, Indigenous Project," *Canadian Journal of Education* 26, no. 2 (2002): 82–95.

26 Frantz Fanon, *The Wretched of the Earth* (New York: Grove Press, 1963), 36.

27 For decolonization as an unsettling practice see Eve Tuck and Wayne Yang, "Decolonization Is Not a Metaphor," *Decolonization: Indigeneity, Education & Society* 1, no. 1 (2012): 1–40. On situating decolonization (and its relationship to Indigenous research and pedagogies) see Linda Tuhiwai Smith, *Decolonizing Methodologies: Research and Indigenous Peoples, Second Edition* (London: Zed Books, 1986); Maureen P. Hogan and Sean A. Topkok, "Teaching Indigenous Methodology and an Iñupiaq Example,"

emerge in connecting to and responsibly engaging other epistemic traditions and theories that might center their narratives on non-human history, connectivity, and kinship.[28] Such traditions might help question how theory and architecture usually perceive themselves—and maybe challenge "we/they" dichotomies and the idea of a First or Western world, together with other, more recent definitions such as the Global North. The approach is very different from the practice of "adding" items of Indigenous knowledge to already-formed teaching curricula—a deeply problematic approach which often results in cultural caricature and inert knowledge, shorn of its context, webs of meaning, and corresponding fields of practice. Of greater interest is the definition of trajectories and orientations as all occurring within a shared history inhabited as a communal experience, albeit from asymmetrical power positions.[29] This implies a qualitative shift of recognition of Indigenous narratives that might represent a critical revision of architectural theory as we know it. This research could constitute a set of alternative theories, against the idea of a single story and a single world order.[30]

Embarking on this new epistemic venture may require more than the use of post-colonial, feminist, and race theory. As Yusaf and Renwick suggest, additional work in this direction also opens research to the experience of non-anthropocentric epistemologies of folk and native cultures—from those of Canadian First Nations to New Zealand Maori peoples.[31] Exploring maps from Ojibwe Indigenous of Canada and Western cultures as metaphors for the territory they represent as well

---

Decolonization: Indigeneity, Education & Society 4, no. 2 (2015): 50–75; and Brian Martin, Georgina Stewart, Bruce Ka'imi Watson, Ola Keola Silva, Jeanne Teisina, Jacoba Matapo and Carl Mika, "Situating Decolonization: An Indigenous dilemma," *Educational Philosophy and Theory* 52, no. 3 (2020): 312–321.

28 On centring tribal knowledge, and on Indigenous and qualitative inquiry see, for example, Margaret Kovach, *Indigenous Methodologies* (University of Toronto Press, 2010).

29 On history and Indigenous self-determination and settler time see Mark Rifkin, *Beyond Settler Time: Temporal Sovereignty and Indigenous Self-determination* (Durham: Duke University Press, 2017).

30 On the idea of the single story see Chimamanda Ngozi Adichie, "The Danger of a Single Story," TED Talks, TEDGlobal 2009 (July 2009), https://www.ted.com/talks/chimamanda_ngozi_adichie_the_danger_of_a_single_story?language=en.

31 Shundana Yusaf, "Decolonizing Architectural Pedagogy," The Ethical Imperative: 106th Annual ACSA Conference, March 15-17, 2018; G. Renwick, "Decolonising Methods: Reflecting upon a Practice-Based Doctorate," in *Thinking Through Art: Reflections on Art as Research*, eds. Katy Macleod and Lin Holdridge (London: Routledge, 2006), 168–84.

as the culture that created them, Turnbull and Watson recognize how these maps define not only diverse understandings of landscape but also religious, ideological, and political domination.[32] The potential products of similar qualitative inquiries and holistic orientations, and a dialogue between more cosmopolitan theories and "non-Cartesian" practices, still needs to be investigated.[33]

How, then, could the architecture curriculum open up to a plurality of theories (or a theory of pluralities)? Attempting to blend together diverse experiences, homogenizing and generalizing Indigeneity, would mean nourishing the colonizing methods and principles of Western-centric research on Indigenous knowledge. The reformation of architectural theory and criticism passes through a horizontal strategy of openness and the acceptance of theories of difference and multiplicity applied to different scales.[34] An holistic study of oral histories, for example, could reveal the non-racial "pluriversity" and communal dimension of the discipline.[35] Addressing the conflict between mainstream scientific theory and the ancestral cosmology of Native Americans, historians such as Deloria recognize that disregarding oral traditions as simple legends would mean sustaining the ethnocentric misconceptions and omissions of settler society.[36] On the other hand, the theorization of the contemporary North American university as a center of knowledge production enmeshed in settler colonialism could help to further understand how we experience the phenomenon—and the entangled triad structure of settler-native-slave—as a current reality,

---

32 David Turnbull and Helen Watson, *Maps Are Territories: Science Is an Atlas: A Portfolio of Exhibits* (University of Chicago Press, 1993), 18–27. On decolonization and theories of the landscape see Julian Raxworthy, "The Landscape of Practices: Decolonizing Landscape Architecture" in *The Routledge Companion to Criticality in Art, Architecture, and Design*, eds. Chris Brisbin and Thiessen Myra (London: Routledge, 2018), 298–314.

33 On qualitative inquiry and holistic orientation in Indigenous settings see Margaret Kovach, *Indigenous Methodologies: Characteristics, Conversations and Contexts* (Toronto: University of Toronto Press, 2009).

34 As Lokko explains, multiplicity has to be applied from the macro to the micro scale, and from urban and architectural design to small-scale art projects. Lesley Naa Norle Lokko, *White Papers, Black Marks: Architecture, Race, Culture* (Minneapolis: University of Minnesota Press, 2000).

35 On the topic of "pluriversity" see A. J. Mbembe, "Decolonizing the University: New Directions," *Arts & Humanities in Higher Education* 15, no.1 (2016): 29–45.

36 Among the writings of the leading Native American scholar and author see Vine Deloria, *God Is Red* (New York: Grosset & Dunlap, 1973); and Vine Deloria, *Red Earth, White Lies: Native Americans and the Myth of Scientific Fact* (New York: Scribner, 1995).

as well as object of investigation.[37] The goal is to recover expertise and power from different ways of knowing and being that the universalist claims of Western systems of knowledge have often discredited. This needs to be done without transforming "Western" knowledge into the "other," normalized and caricaturized, as happens to Indigenous knowledge integrated into academic programs.[38] Instead of simplification for pedagogical purposes, theorists are called to advocate for complexity and richness.

Indeed, the North American educational system has made considerable progress in discussing, for example, globally connected technologies and the environmental crisis from a critical point of view. Investigating the role played by colonization and its violence in the development of digital technologies, for example, Risam explores ways for amplifying voices of resistance.[39] The adoption of new perspectives into the course on history, theory, and criticism might push these and other limits of current discussions, examining, for example, the inability of green architecture and sustainability endeavors to depart from the foundational frameworks responsible for the near annihilation of our globe. After all, the changing climate is an environmental catastrophe in the making for all societies.

Once again, Indigenous knowledge and resistance can teach theorists about connectivity and kinship, as explained by Estes in his discussion on Indigenous opposition at Standing Rock and the Dakota Access Pipeline.[40] Similar recent events and associated environmental

---

37 See, for example, the discussion during the event held in Chicago in October 2019, entitled "Decolonization of Architectural Pasts and Futures." The Conference was organized by Andrew Herscher and Ana María León for SCCP and Ayala Levin and Meredith TenHoor for the Aggregate Architectural History Collaborative, https://chicagoarchitecturebiennial.org/events/decolonization_of_architectural_pasts_and_futures. See also Njoki Wane, "[Re]Claiming my Indigenous Knowledge: Challenges, Resistance, and Opportunities," *Decolonization: Indigeneity, Education & Society* 2, no. 1 (2013): 93–107.

38 On this topic see Brian Martin, Georgina Stewart, Bruce Ka'imi Watson, Ola Keola Silva, Jeanne Teisina, Jacoba Matapo, and Carl Mika, "Situating Decolonization: An Indigenous Dilemma," *Educational Philosophy and Theory* 52, no. 3 (2020): 312–321.

39 See, for example, the book Roopika Risam, *New Digital Worlds: Postcolonial Digital Humanities in Theory, Praxis, and Pedagogy* (Evanston, Illinois: Northwestern University Press, 2018).

40 Nick Estes, *Our History Is the Future: Standing Rock versus the Dakota Access Pipeline, and the Long Tradition of Indigenous Resistance* (New York: Verso, 2019). On this topic see also Eleanor Hayman, "Future Rivers of the Anthropocene or Whose Anthropocene Is It? Decolonising the Anthropocene!,"

disasters, such as the devastating Australian wildfires in 2020, have demonstrated how essential it is that theory rethink the Anthropocene as an epoch in which the human and nonhuman are inextricably linked. Focusing on the connections between nature and culture, Latour claims we must rework our thinking and understanding of nature and culture not as dichotomized objects to be studied by specialists, but as hybrids made possible by the public interaction of people, things, and knowledge.[41] As Haraway develops further, environment and architecture probably require what is called sym-poiesis (or making-with), rather than auto-poiesis (or self-making).[42] Western epistemology rests on a separation between mind and world, and between reason and nature, as an ontological *a priori*. What if we center not the Anthropos but the non-human in the richness of its cosmogony and networked relations? How would this affect the theory of architecture and architecture itself? All these topics should be explored.

If it turns back to its revolutionary origins in the '60s, building on the work of more recent student-driven movements and the scholarly research on connectivity and knowledge on kinship, the course on history, theory, and criticism could be the main engine for broader transformations in the architectural curricula. Within a renewed and more open framework, theory and criticism could be rethought as an ethical and strategic mode of practice in its own right. As Mbembe remembers: "Another site of decolonization is the university classroom... we need to reinvent a classroom without walls in which we are all co-learners."[43] Maybe our role as theorists is to rethink the world while being active parts of it—not above it or outside of it. Or maybe our duty as critics is to reinvent a theory—not only its curriculum—where we genuinely learn from each other, freed from walls and divisions. ●

Decolonization: Indigeneity, Education & Society 6, no. 2 (2018): 77–92; Vanessa Watts, "Indigenous Place-thought & Agency Amongst Humans and Non-humans (First Woman and Sky Woman go on a European World Tour!)," *Decolonization: Indigeneity, Education & Society* 2, no. 1 (2013): 20–34.

41 Bruno Latour and Catherine Porter, *We Have Never Been Modern* (Cambridge, MA: Harvard University Press, 1993).

42 On the concept of sympoiesis see Donna Haraway, "Staying with the Trouble: Anthropocene, Capitalocene and Chthulucene," in *Anthropocene or Capitalocene?: Nature, History, and the Crisis of Capitalism*, ed. Jason Moore, et al. (Chicago: PM Press, 2016), 34–77.

43 Achille Mbembe, "Decolonizing Knowledge and the Question of the Archive," Wits Institute for Social and Economic Research (WISER) (Johannesburg: University of Witwatersrand, 2015), http://wiser.wits.ac.za/system/files/Achille%20Mbembe%20-%20Decolonizing%20Knowledge%20and%20the%20Question%20of%20the%20Archive.pdf.

Globalizing, Expanding, Localizing, Situating: A Plan for an Architectural Theory Revival

Matthew Allen

Imagine that architectural theory is going strong today. And how could it not be? Taking a strictly empirical view, the well-known charts showing precipitously increasing energy expenditure per capita suggest that the furthest reaches of today's tertiary economies—such as the highly-specialized immaterial labor that takes place in PhD programs in architectural theory—ought to be doing well. But is this specialization a liability? Has theory been fragmented and rendered ineffective just as it has been enriched by scholarly sophistication? Younger theorists appear less committed than their predecessors to the exemplary theories of the recent past. Or, rather, the canonical theories—the critical theory of Adorno, the French theory of Foucault, Derrida, and Deleuze, and the architectural theory of Tafuri—are made to coexist, sometimes uncomfortably, with more specialized concerns. Should we take this "subculturalization" of architectural theory as a sign that we need to update our notion of theory itself?

Theory has always been a more capacious term than theorists themselves lead us to believe. According to the Oxford English Dictionary, a theory is "a system of ideas intended to explain something, especially one based on general principles." By the most commonplace definition, theories attempt to understand the world around us using generalizations and abstractions. Before we deconstruct the problematic assumptions of this notion of theory (such as the assumption that *subjects* and *worlds* are somehow cleanly separable), we should note that, at some basic level, everyone makes and uses theories all the time. Theories are essential to thinking, even for the most practically-minded. Press beyond a façade of no-nonsense posturing and you are likely to find a rich ecology of localized theories.

What follows is a thought experiment.[1] Imagine that architecture is made up of a set of partially overlapping subcultures, each with its own interpretive schemas (a.k.a. theories) that allow it to make sense of the world. Following the principle of symmetry from cultural studies, imagine that each of these subcultures has its own "architectural theory" (even if it does not go by that name), and suppose that we should respect the dignity of these theories and try to understand them on their own terms. The premise here is that, counterintuitively, a *global* orientation entails a sensitivity to *local* situations. Identifying, appreciating, and understanding

1 A variant of this essay was first presented at "Theory's History, 196X-199X: Challenges in the Historiography of Architectural Knowledge," a conference hosted by KU Leuven in February 2017. I would like to thank the peer reviewers of the original essay, Hilde Heynen and Sabastiaan Loosen, for their critical comments.

an expanded set of situated theories would thus lead us toward a more globally inclusive view of architecture.

Serious methodological issues arise immediately. If architectural theories are hashed out in the local dialects of subcultures and are thus not fully legible within a broader discourse, how are we to find and interpret evidence of their existence? Do we need to become fluent in their esoteric languages? I outline below another approach: a plan for understanding subcultural theories through situated aesthetic categories. This approach passes through new media theory and into aesthetic theory—to Immanuel Kant by way of Hannah Arendt, then moving on to the contemporary approach to aesthetics suggested by Sianne Ngai and William Reddy. As an example, we can take the subculture made up of computer programmers in architecture around 1970; a small community huddled around computers in architecture schools and the back offices of large corporate firms. *(Figure 1)* While unique and historically specific, in its situatedness it can help us understand how theory operates as a field in our current archipelago of subcultures.

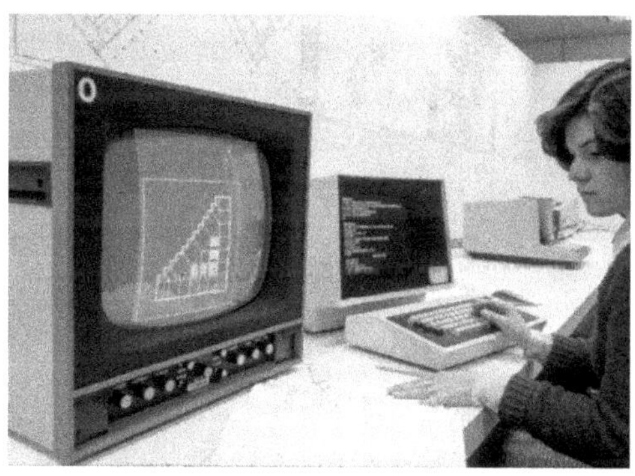

FIG 1:
Computers at SOM's Chicago office, circa 1980.
© SOM, compliments of SOM

THEORY BECOMES SUBCULTURAL

How did architectural theory become subcultural? One way of seeing things is that it was ever thus. Subcultures are just small, situated cultures centering on shared points of reference; Clifford Geertz called them "webs of significance."[2] They are built around intensely felt shared experiences. Subcultures therefore change over time as life-worlds and experiences change. Subcultures are ephemeral; they can disappear.

In the history of Western architecture, the waning of modernism

2 Clifford Geertz, *The Interpretation of Cultures: Selected Essays* (New York: Basic, 1973).

provides the most recent moment when pretenses of a singular culture were abandoned. Chroniclers of architectural theory agree that this happened around 1968.[3] Not coincidentally, this was also the moment when the techno-social dreams of the first computer experts in architecture went from being common sense to seeming embarrassingly out of touch. In other words, the techophilic '60s became the technophobic '70s just as modernism evolved into postmodernism.

It is worth remembering that techno-optimism was a feature of modernism. In a 1957 essay, John Summerson famously suggested that architects would need to reconstruct their discipline around programming—they should give up designing *form* and start to think about organizing *patterns of activity*.[4] A few architects took Summerson's advice to heart. Christopher Alexander wrote software to manipulate architectural programs; Cedric Price seems to have spent most of his time gathering data and drawing diagrams.[5] Two senses of the term "programming" came together in this era. In architecture, programming referred to the practice of organizing functional spaces.[6] In the field of computation, programming referred to the practice of creating software.[7] The craze for "spatial location-allocation" software around 1970 is a tidy example of how these two senses of programming came together: computer programs were written to manipulate architectural programs.[8] *(Figure 2)* Price's Fun Palace (1964), with its computer-

---

3 Joan Ockman, "Introduction," in *Architecture Culture: 1943-1968,* ed. Joan Ockman (New York: Rizzoli, 1993); K. Michael Hays, "Introduction," in *Architecture Theory since 1968,* ed. K. Michael Hays (Cambridge, MA: MIT Press, 1998).

4 John Summerson, "The Case for a Theory of Modern Architecture," *The Journal of the Royal Society of British Architects* 64, no. 8 (June 1957): 307–313.

5 Molly Wright Steenson, *Architectural Intelligence: How Designers and Architects Created the Digital Landscape* (Cambridge, MA: MIT Press, 2017).

6 Architects still refer to "the program" of a building even though the term "programming" never really caught on. Books that promoted programming include, e.g., Benjamin H. Evans and Clarence Herbert Wheeler, *Architectural Programming: Emerging Techniques of Architectural Practice* (AIA, 1969).

7 On the distinction between programming and software engineering, see Federica Frabetti, *Software Theory: A Cultural and Philosophical Study* (Lanham, MD: Rowman & Littlefield, 2014). On the history of programming and the software industry, see Martin Campbell-Kelly, *From Airline Reservations to Sonic the Hedgehog: A History of the Software Industry* (Cambridge, MA: MIT Press, 2003).

8 A bibliography of "the field of computerized location-allocation in environmental design" from 1972 lists 473 relevant publications. Erich

controlled, flexible spaces, went so far as to imagine that computer programming and architectural programming could be the same thing.[9]

In the 1960s, a thriving subculture of programming concentrated wherever there were computers: in technical classes and computer centers at architecture schools, in computer groups at corporate firms, and in a global network of nomadic computer consultants.[10] The tradition of programming in architecture continued as a sub-discipline through the 1970s and '80s, finally rejoining the mainstream with the digital architecture of the '90s.[11] But just as some architects embraced programming in the '60s and '70s, a branch of architectural theory (which I will refer to as "Theory"[12]) gained traction precisely in opposition to it. A famous editorial by Peter Eisenman described how, over the previous centuries, "architecture became increasingly a social or programmatic art," just as Summerson had noted. Contrary to Summerson, however, Eisenman suggested adopting a "non-humanistic attitude" beginning with the "negation of functionalism."[13] Colin Rowe, writing with a different focus but within the same intellectual milieu, equated programming with "naive scientism," and he worried that architects would be sidetracked by an "orgy of expensive but impeccable interdisciplinary collaboration" and end up perpetually "waiting for printout."[14] If Eisenman and Rowe represent the common opinion of Theory circa 1980, the famous debate in those years between Alexander and Eisenman can be seen as the moment when Theory

---

Bunselmeier, *Computerized Location - Allocation. Exchange Bibliography no. 414* (Monticello, IL: Council of Planning Librarians, 1972).

9 Stanley Mathews, "The Fun Palace: Cedric Price's experiment in architecture and technology," *Technoetic Arts* 3, no. 2 (September 2005), 73–91.

10 How exactly this happened is part of a longer story in which – to point out just two factors – corporate modernism and "popular" postmodernism were construed as theoretically shallow and curricula in architecture schools segregated technical and practical courses at a significant distance from courses in history and theory. Matthew Allen, "Prehistory of the Digital: Architecture becomes Programming, 1935-1990," PhD dissertation, 2019.

11 Antoine Picon suggests that before the "digital culture" of the 1990s, architects took part in the "computer culture" of the preceding decades. Antoine Picon, *Digital Culture in Architecture: An Introduction for the Design Professions* (Basel: Birkhäuser, 2010).

12 The other field where "Theory" means roughly the same thing is literary studies. See, e.g., "Theory: Death Is Not the End," *n+1* 2 (Winter 2005).

13 Peter Eisenman, "Post-Functionalism," *Oppositions* 6 (September 1976).

14 Colin Rowe, "Program vs. Paradigm," *The Cornell Journal of Architecture* 2 (1982), 8–19.

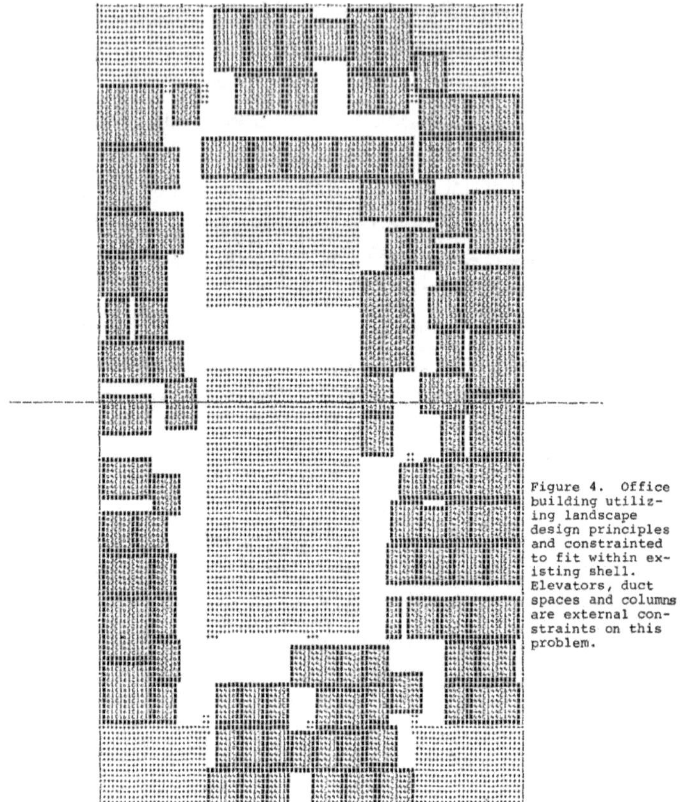

FIG 2:
Office building floorplan designed by Allen Bernholtz and Steve Fosburg, with the help of their software, ALOKAT, 1972.

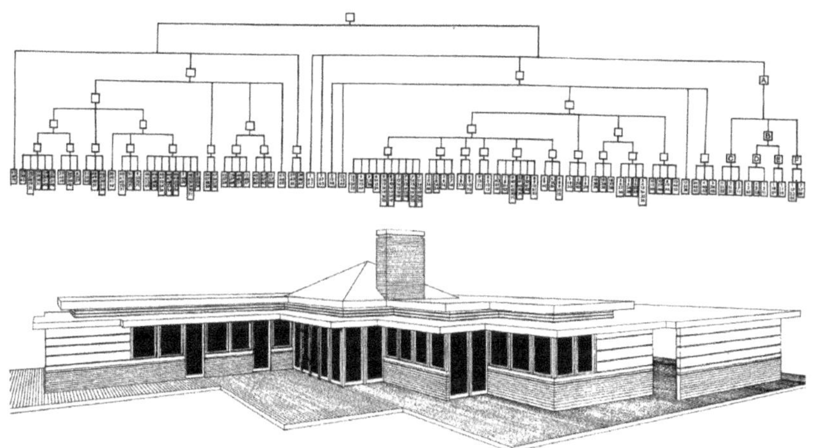

FIG 3:
House designed using software by Christopher Alexander, Allen Bernholtz, and Edward Bierstone, 1966.

"won." While Alexander's buildings might have been pleasant and functional, they were also, as Eisenman argued, boring.[15] *(Figure 3)* Worse, they seemed to be part of an insidious program of social engineering. The buildings advocated by Eisenman, on the other hand, aimed to provoke inhabitants to question their own deeply-held values. In the following decades, this "critical architecture" became associated with Theory, at least in the east coast North American academic context that played such a large role in setting the intellectual standards during this period.[16] Summerson's argument in favor of programming had been tried and tested, and it had been repudiated.

However true the forgoing historical sketch may be, it certainly must be qualified. The Theory that repudiated programming—embodied, for example, in the essays collected in K. Michael Hays's *Architecture Theory since 1968*—belongs to a particular lineage of Frankfurt School critical theory, and as such it views programming (in both the architectural and computer science senses) as a force of instrumentalism and normalization. Theorists in this lineage typically suspect that the rationalism required to conform to the dictates of computer logic or functional requirements is akin to totalitarianism.[17] In fact, they seem to have regarded a particular *habit of thought* as the true enemy. When Theodor Adorno moved to Los Angeles, he saw authoritarian thinking everywhere—in classrooms, in jazz music, in newspaper astrology columns.[18] North American consumer culture and technocracy were certainly forces to be reckoned with. Hence the urgent need for opposition, particularly from the intellectual bastions of the East Coast—and particularly from "autonomous" activities such as music, painting, and the formalist architecture that aligned itself with avant-garde artistic

---

15 Christopher Alexander and Peter Eisenman, "Contrasting concepts of harmony in architecture," *Lotus International* 40, no. 67 (1983), 60–68.

16 See, e.g., Louis Martin, "History, Theory, Criticism," and Mary McLeod, "1968-1990: The End of Innocence: From Political Activism to Postmodernism," in *Architecture School: Three Centuries of Educating Architects in North America*, e.d. Joan Ockman (Cambridge, MA: MIT Press, 2012).

17 An extreme version can be seen by bringing together Hannah Arendt's "Crisis in Culture" and *Eichmann in Jerusalem*: her arguments set up a certain affinity between the philistine who approaches art in terms of use value and Adolf Eichmann, the Nazi officer who perpetrated genocide under the guise of bureaucratic logistics. (Arendt was not part of the Frankfurt School, though she shared many concerns with them and was in the same generation as, for instance, Adorno.) Hannah Arendt, *Between Past and Future: Six Exercises in Political Thought* (New York: Viking, 1961); and *Eichmann in Jerusalem: A Report on the Banality of Evil* (New York: Viking, 1963).

18 See Theodor Adorno, *The Stars Down to Earth* (Abingdon: Routledge, 2001).

production.

While suspicion regarding programming still lingers today, we should note that Alexander and other proponents of programming were not naive functionaries. The committee for Alexander's 1963 dissertation was comprised of a political scientist, an architect and industrial designer, and a cognitive psychologist. Though not mainstream within architecture today, his ideas formed the basis of the "design methods" movement, and his theory of "design patterns" is still a respectable approach in computer science.[19] Alexander was not only highly theoretical, but also strongly polemical: he offered a critique of what he saw as the dominant contemporary ways of doing architecture, and a path beyond modernism that appears, in retrospect, to have been prescient.

From a historical perspective, it is clear that such situated theories did not disappear even after they were excluded from Theory. My argument here does not apply only to the subculture of programming. Fragmentation and subculturalization were hallmarks of the postmodern period. Hays, for one, has suggested that the 1960s saw the end of the illusion of a single shared "architecture culture," and that the 1970s was the beginning of an era of fragmentary, insular subcultures.[20] Once the distinction between *Theory* and *theories* is set aside, we can begin to locate and appreciate the situated knowledge that thrived within each of these subcultures.

LOCATING SUBCULTURAL THEORIES

Tricky methodological questions arise once we agree that theories can exist even when they are not articulated in the terms of a hegemonic discourse. How are we to find and interpret theories that are not spelled out in conventional theoretical prose? A postulate of new media theory can help us identify these situated theories. The postulate is that *practices precede concepts*.[21] The usual example is that people made marks of one sort or another long before the concept of "writing" solidified.[22]

19 The transfer from architecture to computer science was christened with Erich Gamma et al., *Design Patterns: Elements of Reusable Object-Oriented Software* (Boston: Addison-Wesley, 1994).

20 K. Michael Hays, "Introduction," x.

21 Bernhard Siegert, "Introduction: Cultural Techniques, or, The End of the Intellectual Postwar in German Media Theory," *Cultural Techniques: Grids, Filters, Doors, and Other Articulations of the Real* (New York: Fordham University Press, 2015).

22 Thomas Macho, "Zeit und Zahl: Kalender- und Zeitrechnung als Kulturtechniken," in *Bild, Schrift, Zahl*, eds. Sybille Krämer and Horst

Likewise, assemblages of processors and input and output devices were being used before "the interactive computer" or "computer-aided design" or "digital modeling" became stable concepts.[23] If theories are situated in contexts of practice, cultural techniques stand out as figures of knowledge that mark these theories.

This line of reasoning poses more problems, however. Does every instance of practice engender its own theories? If so, then what is the basis for believing that a theory is shared among a subcultural group? Following the approach of Bruno Latour, we could begin by looking at the means by which ideas spread – at "immutable mobiles" (marks on paper) and how they circulate, binding people together.[24] *(Figure 4)* We could take a step back from interpreting the *meaning* of text and look instead at the *distribution patterns* of marks of all kinds. We could proceed from there to map commonalities and conventions in words and images. We would ask of these visual and textual conventions not what they signify, but what they *do* (or what people have done with them).

Cultural techniques thus play a mediating role between practices and theories. Traditionally, aesthetics has been seen as playing a similar mediating role, translating subjective judgements of singular things into the shared values of a "community of taste."[25] Commenting on Immanuel Kant's aesthetic philosophy and updating it for the mid-twentieth century, Hannah Arendt emphasized the specifically *political* role of aesthetics. Aesthetic judgements, Arendt says,

> share with political opinions that they are persuasive; the judging person—as Kant says quite beautifully—can only 'woo the consent of everyone else' in the hope of coming to an agreement with him eventually [...] Culture and politics, then, belong together because it is not knowledge

---

Bredekamp (Paderborn: Wilhelm Fink, 2003).

23 Michael Mahoney argues that the various devices that have been lumped into the category of "computers" should be disaggregated and approached through the histories of the groups that used them. Michael Mahoney, "The histories of computing(s)," *Interdisciplinary Science Reviews* 30, no. 2 (June 2005).

24 Bruno Latour, "Visualization and Cognition: Drawing Thing Together," *Knowledge and Society: Studies in the Sociology of Culture Past and Present,* Vol. 6, eds. Robert Alun and Henrika Kuklick (Stamford, CT: Jai Press, 1986).

25 Charlton Payne, "Kant's Parergonal Politics: The *Sensus Communis* and the Problem of Political Action," in *Kant and the Concept of Community,* eds. Charlton Payne and Lucas Thorpe (Rochester, NY: University of Rochester Press, 2011).

> or truth which is at stake, but rather judgment and decision, the judicious exchange of opinion about the sphere of public life and the common world, and the decision [regarding] what manner of action is to be taken in it, as well as to how it is to look henceforth, what kind of things are to appear in it.[26]

Expanding on Arendt's insight, we could say that decisions about which *theories* are allowed to appear in shared life are also aesthetic judgements. They are not about knowledge per se, but about what knowledge is allowed to circulate.

Appreciating subcultural theories is similar to appreciating subcultural aesthetics. In the quotation above, Arendt agrees with Kant that the moment of aesthetic judgement is when taste becomes public—it is when we put ourselves in the place of others, imagine what they would think, and try to formulate a judgement that they would agree with. The problem is that Arendt, like most philosophers of aesthetics, assumes that it makes sense to talk about "everyone," "the public," "universal" judgements, and a singular "culture." For Arendt, Greece and Rome stand in for all human values. She worries about how the singular culture she so evidently loves (Western culture) appears to be in the process of dissolution under the pressure of mass culture (which, she says, is not culture at all but "entertainment"—what culture becomes when it is instrumentalized). Writing on the heels of several decades of catastrophe, critics like Arendt tended to think in terms of enormous existential conundrums. "Mankind" and "culture" were universal values to be defended, and they were often seen in terms of sweeping binary paradigms: culture vs. civilization (Paul Ricoeur and Kenneth Frampton), autonomy vs. instrumentality (Adorno and Eisenman), etc. Having now passed through a several-decades-long celebration of multiculturalism, these champions of a singular, universal "culture" look more and more like relics of the Cold War.

While the Kantian aesthetics of Arendt aim toward the universal, why not update aesthetics? Can we imagine aesthetic judgements to be *shared* but not universal? One approach is to see aesthetic schema as analogous to emotions. The realm of emotions, like the realm of aesthetics, has traditionally been understood as "universal," but with a little effort we can see how emotions are always culturally situated.[27]

---

26 Arendt, *Between Past and Future,* 222–223.

27 For an overview, see William Reddy, *The Navigation of Feeling: A Framework for*

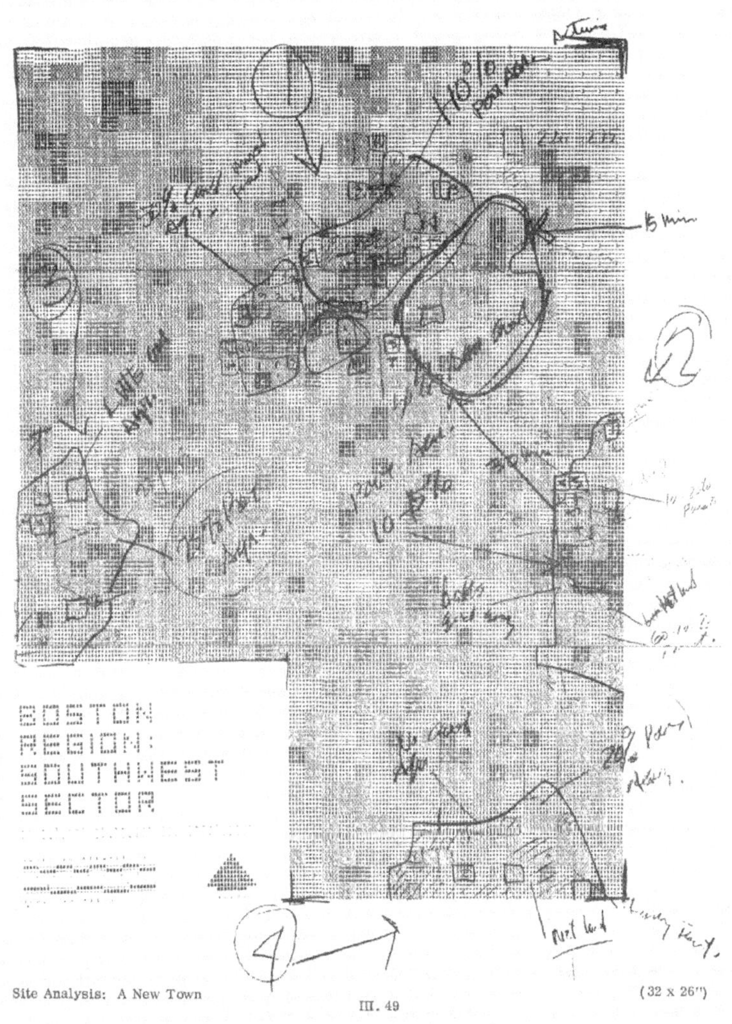

FIG 4:
Notes on a regional analysis mapping printout from the program SYMAP, produced in a course by Carl Steinitz, 1967. Courtesy of the Frances Loeb Library. Harvard University Graduate School of Design.

William Reddy describes emotions as "bundles of loosely-connected thought material" that we come to name and categorize through a long process of enculturation. The connotations of and boundaries between emotional schema depend on our upbringing in a specific culture. Once a system of emotional schemas is in place in our head, it provides templates for rapid response to situations encountered in everyday experience. Reddy shows how this updated understanding of emotions is useful for historians who find themselves navigating between relativism and universalism when making judgments about oppression or freedom in foreign places and times.

Aesthetic categories, like emotions, can be understood as "bundles of loosely-connected thought material" that we share with others and use to make quick judgements. Once we see aesthetic judgements as not universal but *subcultural,* a finer grain of aesthetic categories becomes apparent. Arendt, like Kant, generally limited her discussion to beauty. Kant also wrote about the sublime,[28] and Rozenkratz added ugliness to the repertoire.[29] Writing about the world of post-industrial labor, Sianne Ngai adds the cute, the zany, and the interesting.[30] In a significant update to aesthetic theory, Ngai argues that

> our aesthetic experience is always mediated by a finite if constantly rotating repertoire of aesthetic categories [...], which are by definition conceptual as well as affective and tied to historically specific forms of communication and collective life.[31]

As a slightly absurd example of what this expanded cast of aesthetic categories might look like, we could turn to Benjamin Buchloh's analysis of the fine-tuned aesthetic work done by conceptual artists in the postwar period.[32] In order of appearance, he lists:

---

the History of Emotions (Cambridge, UK: Cambridge University Press, 2004), particularly "Part I: What Are Emotions?"

28 Immanuel Kant, *Beobachtungen über das Gefühl des Schönen und Erhabenen* (1764).

29 Karl Rosenkrantz, *Die Aesthetik des Hässlichen* (1853).

30 Sainne Ngai, *Our Aesthetic Categories: Zany, Cute, Interesting* (Cambridge, MA: Harvard University Press, 2015).

31 Sainne Ngai, "Our Aesthetic Categories," *PMLA* 125, no. 4 (October 2010), 948.

32 Benjamin Buchloh, "Conceptual Art 1962-1969: From the Aesthetic of Administration to the Critique of Institutions," *October* 55 (Winter 1990), 105–143.

the aesthetic of administration
the aesthetic of the speech act
the aesthetic of linguistic convention and legalistic arrangements
the aesthetic of the handcrafted original
the aesthetic of administrative and legal organization and institutional validation
the aesthetic of contemplative experience
the aesthetic of mural painting
the aesthetic of Conceptual Art
the aesthetic of permutation
the aesthetic of the studio
the aesthetic of production and consumption
the aesthetic of declaration and intention
the aesthetic of the newly established power of administration
the aesthetic of anonymity

Each of these aesthetic categories served as a shorthand that artists mobilized to situate themselves within a particular artistic milieu. With such a nuanced terrain of aesthetic categories to structure his analysis, Buchloh has no problem mapping the theories of the artists in question. The aesthetic of anonymity, for example, is related to a theory that valorizes anonymous techniques over genius authorship. The former (the aesthetic schema) can be used to locate and begin the work of critically unpacking the latter (the theory).

Returning now to programmers in architecture, it is clear that they had their own aesthetic subculture. In 1970, there were very few people who had used computers, and with no widespread experience of computation, there were no common shorthands around which to build a broad aesthetic discourse. Instead, wireframe images pointed toward localized theories of the deep structure of architecture and the expertise required to manipulate it. *(Figure 5)*

Screenshots emerged from theories of interactivity and simulation that matched contemporary architectural phenomenology. The clunky pixelization of chain printer drawings was developed alongside theories of data and visualization and countercultural ideals of hacking and democracies of information. Each of these was a new aesthetic category that could be used to gesture toward shared theories, but that only made sense within a small subculture.

This suggests a role for aesthetics in the revitalization of architectural theory: to provide an initial set of categories with which to describe concerns and concepts in a way that is schematic and shared but not universal. Confronted with practices and images that seem to be related to some theoretical content within a subculture, we could begin by identifying a set of aesthetic categories at work. We could then elaborate the thought material with which they are associated. Extrapolating the systematicity of this thought material will lead us to theories. In this way, aesthetic categories stand as figures of knowledge that mark situated theories.

One final possibility haunts this discussion: should architectural theory be understood as a meta-theory—theory about the many subcultural theories architects happen to imagine? Is there one theory to rule them all, a grand theoretical Architecture behind the vernacular discourses? Such delusions of grandeur reassert themselves with surprising frequency. I find them unsatisfying: they devolve into discussions of cultural politics, not architecture. I recommend humility. To talk about architecture is to talk about peculiar beliefs within subcultures. This is where the action is.

So perhaps my plan for an architectural theory revival begins with a change in optics. Rather than seeing the theorist as the expert, the architect, and the arbiter of Theory, we should begin by appreciating the ecology of theories teeming all around us. Theory is already thriving. The theorist should *cultivate* theory, not construct it. As Sanford Kwinter suggested some time ago, advanced thinking in architecture is a pastoral art.[33] The work to be done involves nudging people in the right direction along lines they are already pursuing. •

33 Sanford Kwinter, "The Building, the Book, and the New Pastoralism," *ANY* 9 (November/December 1994).

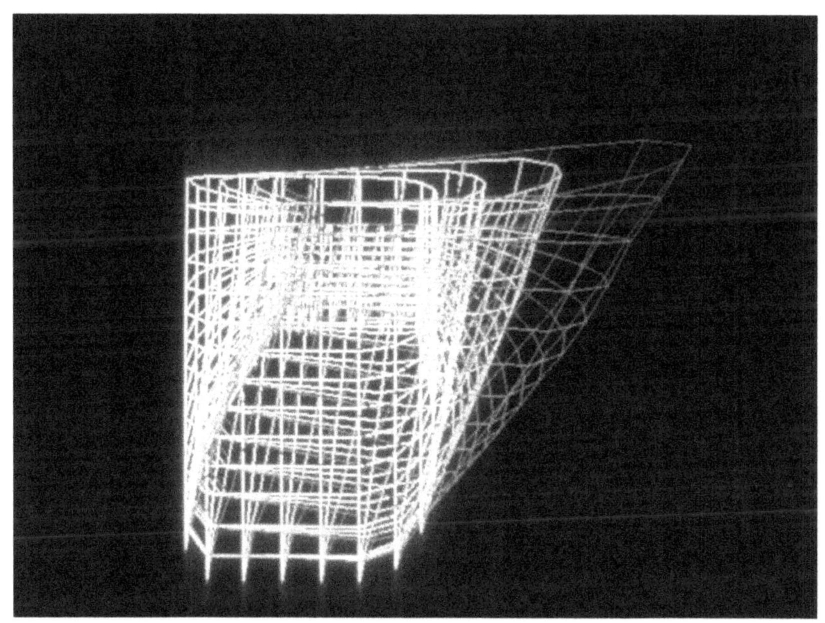

FIG 5:
Structural analysis of a highrise building by SOM, produced using their software, SDMS.
© SOM, compliments of SOM

A Rough Sketch for a Model of Practice for a Hypothetical Discourse

Antonio Furgiuele

The core architectural practices within academia need to be critiqued to provide necessary space to be theorized anew. These practices have the ability to directly affect and propel larger global professional practices.[1] To critically engage ideas of 'The Global,' architectural academia needs to find agency in its practices that are spatialized and enacted locally.[2]

The period following 2008 was marked by successive waves of creative destruction, challenging models of global knowledge and practice and upending established economic, political, informational, and environmental models.[3] For global publics, the challenges to these

---

1 The title is a reference to "A Rough Sketch for a Sample Lesson for a Hypothetical Course" a presentation by Charles Eames, Alexander Girard, and George Nelson, (UCLA, 1953), which was subsequently transformed into the film "A Communication Primer" (1953). The 'Rough Sketch' played with communicative practices to challenge the dogmas of education in order that it "decompartmentalize" specialized scientific knowledge and render it accessible to other design communities. As Charles Eames stated, it was "an attempt to determine how much information could be given to a class in sixty-minutes." He described its goal was to replace the conventional lecture with new teaching techniques, to promote the "break down of barriers between fields of learning... making people a little more intuitive... [and] increasing communication between people and things."

2 Models are composed of a series of variables and are arranged into an organization or network that can affect or render intelligible virtual and material effects. Models provide an underlying theoretical structure of variables to understand relationships and can be used both analytically and speculatively. They are instruments to understand and perform on environments that aide in development, regulation, management, and control. Used by institutions, groups, and individuals to engage complex economic, political, and social relationships, recent shifts within technologies, the era of 'big data,' coupled with socioeconomic changes have allowed for concurrent models to be both challenged, rethought, and overturned. Paul Mason, "It's Time to Junk the Flawed Economic Models That Make the World a Dangerous Place," *The Guardian*, September 19, 2016, https://www.theguardian.com/commentisfree/2016/sep/19/its-time-to-junk-the-flawed-economic-models-that-make-the-world-a-dangerous-place.

3 The systemic shifts abound. From the US economic crisis, the Arab Spring, the rise of popular movements opposed to authoritarian regimes, #MeToo, Black Lives Matter, the swing to global populism, and the new catastrophic climatic projections—combined with the industrialization and wide-scale availability of cloud-based technologies—came new modes for global and local governance. For additional information about 'models' as foundational to theoretical discourse, see Vilém Flusser, "On the Crisis of Our Models," trans. Erik Eisel, in *Flusser, Writings*, ed. Andreas Ströhl (Minneapolis: University of Minnesota Press, 2006), 75–84.

models and others have created a tsunami of uncertainty that has provoked opposing reactions from wild euphoria to extreme melancholy.

Compounded by the accelerated production and consumption of ideas and 'content,' the public thirsts for something like theory to make principled sense out of the shifting ground beneath its feet. Any cogent theory behaves like a force-multiplier on belief systems for both individuals and their global villages.[4] Access to massive platforms of information has rendered theory a prime discourse for both ideological demigods who want to 'Make *Everything* Great Again' and a generation of designers anxious to find principled relationships in their work and practices of everyday life.[5]

Our architectural disciplinary models, both pedagogical and professional, are tethered to these larger global models. Recent shifts within these models have directly impacted society's changing values, practices, and forms of agency. The means to produce and consume the built environment have wildly changed, while methods to teach students about architecture have largely stayed the same. Unlike professional practice, which is quick to surf the forces of paradigm shifts or seek financial ruin, architectural academia has made curricular changes while retaining its core disciplinary practices.[6] The methods of

---

4 Theories can take various forms, as diagrams, principles, schemas, maps, and models. They propel how discourses, systems, environments, and beings can be understood and constructed or changed. The focus of theory falls between understanding (logic, systems, recognition, representation) and ability (techniques, methods, practices).

5 Make 'Everything' Great Again, is a reference to the populist slogan *Make America Great Again*. This phrase, associated with US President Donald Trump, needs to be extended, ideologically, to include others that instrumentalize nostalgia for institutional or individual power, which includes select academics. Forms of increased disciplinary anxiety, in the past ten years, about the importance, value, and relevance of architectural practices and modes of production allow certain academic camps to instrumentalize history through forms of theory to make architecture great again—most often felt through the adherence to dogmatic pedagogy and academic practices. The focus here in this text is to position the key elements of architectural academia for educators, students and emergent architects to incorporate into their 'practice of every day life.' This statement is a direct reference to theorist Michel de Certeau and his seminal text, *The Practice of Every Day Life* (1984).

6 The term "surf" is used as a mode of navigating socio-economic forces: to utilize the overwhelming forces of cultural change to propel oneself in a direction, to harness its energy. This is in contradistinction to notions of "resistance," which acts to stop large systemic changes, often with the

instruction and evaluation remain largely the same, and the practices that underpin architectural academia are painfully dogmatic and only serve to stifle global possibilities. At the core of architectural academia is an increasingly formalistic and technocratic method of thinking which incentivizes atomization of expertise that is often technical and focused on individual research. This shift has come at a price, as it downplays the presence of historical, theoretical, and critical discourses.

Our dominant educational practices are built upon a powerful and outdated belief system. For example, design studios are modeled largely on the logic of *composition* or *research,* which requires thorough critical analysis. Most entry-level design studios fetishize spatial composition, often described with names that reinforce a culture of cool.[7] They aggrandize formal autonomy and forsake almost all else. Compositional thinking, carried over from the Beaux-Arts educational model, is now measured against and driven by global image culture. Composition is intensified to maximize its ability to be imaged, trafficked, and quickly consumed. The contemporary interest in form has produced hyper-compositions; form is primarily understood and valued by its ability to be transmitted solely as an image with the ability to create a global image footprint and, by extension, global audiences.[8] Perhaps unsurprisingly, composition fits well within the structures of the contemporary information age. Valorized by the conspicuous consumption of distinct objects and an obsolescence of form, the hyper-composition divorces itself from context and purports to have no other environment than its image-context.[9] Those who pursue this line of creative inquiry reinforce the mythical starchitect system, encouraging objects that purport to have the status of buildings but have no ethical relationship to their surroundings.

---

aid of collectives, multitudes, or aggregates.

7 A reference to the tendency of academics to describe their studios and design pedagogies with names that allow for maximum social media impact via polemical provocation, allowing them to accrue both cultural capital and institutional legitimacy.

8 Contemporary architectural groups like *Possible Mediums* have newly championed formal and compositional aesthetics. While much of their work has been affiliated with a re-positioning of the neo-avant-garde and post-modern architects, it largely instrumentalizes their aesthetic agenda.

9 The developed term 'image-context' refers to the total set of relationships embedded within the image: the image content, the software commands, and its techniques. This context, while integral to the meaning of the image, may not have the same set of attributes as a physical or material environment.

Other studios fetishize individual *research* as a means to tailor a couture-curriculum to a number of students with their own select interests.[10] The research studio aligns itself with contemporary internet culture, privileging a curatorial approach to constructing architectural consequence. Within this model, students move from gathering information to establishing a network of relationships, then using aggregate information to build a set of principles to then govern these relationships, and voilà, theory emerges for the student as a schema, map, diagram, set of rules, or a model of how something works. The increased popularity of the research-studio has propelled the contemporary architectural appetite for "theory," since it allows information to be selectively configured into a principled framework, and for the select few, provides an increase of cultural capital. Theory, here, detached from history and criticism, registers its contempt for discourse and can never make claims to be productively discursive because it has no ground from which to operate. This form of research further contributes to the compartmentalization of theory away from its well-positioned allies, architectural history and architectural criticism.

Other elements within architecture education also need focused criticism and new models of practice, from our overly techno-managerial way of thinking about *sustainability* and the way it propels LEED Platinum beliefs in a positivist building science to our stagnant systems of representation.[11] *Orthography*, the dominant system of representational thinking, carried over from the machine age, has conditioned our modes of thought, disciplinary terms, and technical instruments. While systems of orthography are embedded into software and daily interactions, it obfuscates the understanding of digital media as it constantly refers back to the technical functions of parallel rulers, "T" squares, lines, and

---

10 The research model also props up precarious labor relationships within academia, by allowing adjunct and full time faculty to frame their research interests into the studio and advance their own projects through the labor of students. The pressure on this model has only increased in recent years, as has the prescriptive structure of research studios. While it allows faculty to convert their expertise into a pedagogy, shifting academic tenure systems, a diminishing amount of full time faculty positions, and the changing publishing industry all increase collective desire to allow theses studios to produce work. These concurrent shifts within academia have propelled the research studio to be more prescriptive, focusing on the transfer of information.

11 Kiel Moe, "Compelling Yet Unreliable Theories of Sustainability," *Journal of Architectural Education* 60, no. 4 (May 2007): 24–30. See Kiel Moe's work on the difference between intensivity and extensivity.

layers, and not to the vector and raster units that compose the visible spectrum of digital imaging. Orthographic representational thinking confuses an understanding of the conditions of medium with its potential, which is one composed of electronic or digital signals.[12] As our dominant mode of representation, it highlights our dogmatic way of thinking about the medium of representation, which is evidenced in the ways we as a discipline speak about it (as drawing), think about it (as authored), project through it (2D-3D), and continue to privilege it (as romantic modernists), with little regard to actual medium specificity.

It is necessary to rethink the core of architectural education as it extends to our evaluative discourse about what is produced within the arena of *the crit*. The crit feeds the mythos of the starchitect; it is the famed means of evaluation, in which a student stands alone in front of a seated 'jury' (group of academics and architects), to defend the logic and decisions made within their design work. The crit allows all emerging architects to have their fifteen minutes on center stage to command the discourse or be consumed by it. It propels most students to establish architectural work as a defense, in quasi-legal terms, through scientistic representations. Likewise, perhaps unsurprisingly, the *charrette*—the period of time before a project is due where architecture students are constantly in studio, working beyond the point of mental and physical exhaustion—needs to be critiqued for the way it builds a normative culture of exploitation. The origin of the term, a reference to the romanticized little donkey chart that was pulled by an overworked 19th-century student within the École des Beaux-Arts, should no longer be the symbol of architectural academia. This twisted form of Beaux-Arts-tradition-as-Protestant-work-ethic is passed off as a 'right of passage' and source of disciplinary pride. This masochistic practice results in systemic abuse as an accepted part of professional practice, integrated smoothly with the financialization of global architectural practice.

Teaching theory today demands attention to these models of architectural practice and the dogmatic norms they enforce. An architectural theory education can stay quietly within the domain of curating more nuanced global content, which can be achieved rather easily with our new information technologies that allow for greater curricular competency, access, and exchange. The medium of education, and the models that propel how architecture education

---

12 See John May on orthography: John May, "Everything Is Already an Image," *Log* 40 (Spring/Summer 2017).

works, must be the first stop to localize the spatial practices of the global. For this to find necessary discourse, a significant era of criticism of architectural education is necessary to open up critical spaces and build new pedagogical models. Our ability, as educators and theorists, is to find agency in the global that is contingent on spatial practices of everyday architectural life.[13]

Architectural academia's pedagogic models, maintained by a handful of (self-serving) camps, have ruled for too long. These architectural histories, fueled by necessary criticisms, serve to propel avenues of theory that have just begun to find their way into select curricula.[14]

CAMPS, CLICHÉS, AND CONVENTIONS[15]

The following academic elements underpin pedagogy: *composition/research* (studio curricula); *sustainability* (science and belief systems); *orthography* (representational media); *and the crit and the charrette* (systems of evaluation and discipline) establish a set of powerfully influential architectural norms and practices. These elements prop up architectural academia's major camps and convenient clichés, the internal structures of professional practice, and, by extension, evidence structures of power.

Provided sustained (economic and political) pressure and time, two large camps typically emerge within global systems of practice. These binary camps allow for the staging of debates, produce a requisite strawman to villainize, and provide a necessary 'choice' between opposing parties. This two-product, two-processor, or two-party system is evidenced in the opposition of Coke versus Pepsi, and their staged 'cola wars'; Mac versus PC, and their computer wars; and of course, in the US, by the Democrats versus Republicans, and their continuous political charade. The discipline of architecture can find comfort in the

13 Many architectural institutions that shape academia deserve a focused review outside the scope of this essay: National Architecture Accreditation Board (NAAB) and National Council of Architectural Registration Boards (NCARB) wield important influence that stifles higher education experimentation, risk-taking, and increasingly propels academic bureaucratization.

14 See John May on the crit: John May, "Under Our Present Conditions, Our Dullness Will Intensify," *Project Journal* 3 (2014).

15 The 'Triple C' of *Camps, Clichés, and Conventions* is an inversion of, and oblique reference to 'Triple O' (Object-Oriented Ontology) and its difficulty in acknowledging the influence of structures of institutional power within its philosophy.

fact that we, too, have two signature camps: *The Formalists' Camp* and *The Systems Camp*.

THE FORMALISTS' CAMP[16]

The Formalists use techniques to break down legible figural compositions into many constituent parts connected via diagrams, syntax, deep structure, and of course so-called parametricism.[17] While form is typically understood as having extensive or intensive qualities, *The Formalists* fetishize extensivity: mass, volume, and other formal properties that can be easily subdivided, numerated, and computed.[18] This allows them to have almost no relationship with energy, context, environmental systems, and rarely any interesting use of materials. By today's global standards they have almost no relationship with environmental ethics. Most presentations by *The Formalists* articulate dazzling forms through elaborate processes, and espouse the truly powerful politics of ~~beautiful~~ rational forms. They are part of a legacy that fetishizes a semantics of form which supports the simple alibi that aesthetic compositions can obfuscate almost anything, 'critically.'[19]

The Other Formalists make use of everyday diagrams, collage, montage, duck/shed diagrams, paranoid critical method, and theories that profess the possibilities of BIGness.[20] Like *The Formalists* they find ways to play with form, but instead of looking at Critical Theory (with a capital 'C') to extract value from the meaning of form, they use the quotidian, Other forms, or what some might call cultural theory (with a small 'c'). Within the culture industry *The Other Formalists* differ from *The Formalists* in that they position their forms as disciplinary Others—ordinary things or extra-ordinary places (e.g. Las Vegas, Lagos, Downtown Athletic Clubs,

---

16 These architecture camps seem to have formed sometime during the Second Industrial Revolution in the 1850s, with the advancement of structures of cultural capital and advanced socio-technological systems.

17 While 'The Formalists' encompass and propel The Global, they are epitomized by the following characters: Rudolph Wittkower, Colin Rowe, Peter Eisenman, and Zaha Hadid/Patrik Schumacher. Many other architects, historians, and theorists could be located as within or reacting to these two camps. The sheer simplicity of this section is to provide the requisite polemical position.

18 Extensive properties are often held in contradistinction to intensive properties: flows of temperature, pressure, and densities.

19 Joseph Godlewski, "The Absurd Alibi," The Plan Journal 0 (March 2016): 7–14.

20 'The Other Formalists' are epitomized by some of the following characters: Robert Venturi and Denise Scott Brown, Office for Metropolitan Architecture (OMA), and Bjarke Ingels Group (BIG).

Ducks, Sheds, Salvador Dali, shopping malls, junk, etc.) in contrast to *The Formalists* who find formal criticality in cliché centers of critical theory (e.g. critical theory, philosophy, humanism, post-humanism, etc.). *The Other Formalists,* keeping to their name, also fetishize extensivity, which makes most of their buildings excellent as images, as provocative polemics, while being simultaneously horrible to heat and almost impossible to maintain, leaving their clients with leaky avant-garde architecture.

THE SYSTEMS CAMP

The System Generalists often make use of ideas like scientific management, mass production, standardization, general systems, and synergy.[21] They don't use terms like structuralism or post-structuralism unless referring to advanced structural systems, which they like to invent. They tend to be branded as the quirky technophiles who find joy in seeking out patents. Their confidence in technology is quasi-utopian, and their reliance upon systems thinking absolute. Because of the size of their offices, or their ethics, they never seemed to 'go corporate,' which keeps their own managerial systems from becoming too big to fail.

THE SYSTEM TECHNO-MANAGERIALISTS

The System Techno-Managerialists instrumentalize ideas such as scientific management, standardization, and general systems in the architectural office to help professional practice position itself within late capitalism: viva the architectural corporation.[22] One important system they developed is the organization of offices in multiple time-zones such that architectural production can be continuous by allowing them to circumnavigate the globe. This provides a new method to 'fast-track' projects, by taking advantage of time zone differences and strategically managing offices to continuously produce architecture with no 'down-time': the perpetual global charrette. By implementing systems ideas in the management of the office, they created a new era of efficiency to develop supersized projects and transform the architectural office into a sublime machinic force.

Architecture's central myopic theoretical focus has revolved around a single branch of Critical Theory—semiotics, structuralism, and post-

---

21 'The System Generalists' are epitomized by: Reyner Banham, Cedric Price, Buckminster Fuller, Frei Otto, and Renzo Piano.

22 '*The System Techno-Managerialists*' are epitomized by: SOM, AECOM, HOK, and Gensler.

structuralism. While almost all the discussions revolved around 'texts' (signs, symbols, syntax, and deconstruction), this mode of critical inquiry had little-to-no interest in media (or mediation), matter (or energy), geography (or cultural politics), or technology (or technics). Over the past thirty years, while other disciplines built significant relationships around the above discourses, architecture's primary avenue of critical inquiry was linguistic and semantic. Associated fields that have produced significant theories and discourse in the past thirty years have privileged an understanding of global technicity and its effects: science technology studies, media studies, geography, material studies, and anthropology are the best arenas to quickly catch up. Our collective disciplinary interests seem to only have the requisite bandwidth to focus on these two camps, aesthetic *Formalists* or techno-managerial *Systematists,* and all of their dramas, staged debates, and conversations.

The increased speed of information exchange has given even more importance to camps, clichés, and conventions. Our culture of expediency demands that we are neatly 'like' this or 'like' that, and this demand prevails even within our most celebrated institutions. They have become, perversely, our most commonly used instruments to position theory, concepts, and ideas. Our most celebrated camps, *The Formalists* and *The Systematists,* with their countless global progenerators, seem to revel in an architectural institutional model that further propels, uncritically, the elements of *composition/research—orthography—sustainability—the crit—the charrette.* For theory to engage the global, it must find agency in the local—in the institutions and spatial practices that compose architectural academia and its educational models.[23] We must be willing to acknowledge that our camps, clichés, and conventions, wielding enormous disciplinary influence, perpetuate these dogmatic elements of architectural academia. We must allow critical theory, freed from its orthodoxy of language games, to operate on local material practices. Our ability to render new forms of agency to the global lies in the everyday spatial practices we perform and the spaces we occupy. ●

---

23 *Experiments in Pedagogy,* taught at the Massachusetts Institute of Technology in Fall 2018 and developed by Mark Jarzombek, Ana Miljacki, Rania Ghosn, and Caitlin Mueller, developed a model of education around types of pedagogic experiments that directly operated on academic conventions and clichés. While nascent, it allowed for the small and important glimpse of a pedagogic model that could operate within—and on—the school curriculum. The model evidences a new set of academic practices.

Biographies

JOSEPH BEDFORD

Joseph Bedford is Assistant Professor of History and Theory at Virginia Tech. He holds a PhD in architecture from Princeton University, degrees in Architecture from Cambridge University and the Cooper Union, and was the recipient of the 2008–2009 Rome Scholarship at the British School in Rome. He is the founding director of the *Architecture Exchange*, has taught at Princeton and Columbia University, and has published in *ARQ*, *AA Files*, *OASE* and *Log*.

JEREMY LECOMTE

Jeremy Lecomte is Associate Professor at L'École Nationale Supérieure d'Architecture de Versailles. He holds a PhD in architecture from the University of Manchester, as well as an Mphil in cultural studies from Goldsmiths, University of London, and an MA in political philosophy from the École des Hautes Études en Sciences Sociales, Paris. He is cofounder of the art and theory journal *Glass Bead*, https://www.glass-bead.org/. In parallel to his research and teaching activities, he collaborates regularly with artists and architects on different exhibition and building projects."

GINGER NOLAN

Ginger Nolan is Assistant Professor of Architectural History and Theory at the University of Southern California. She has published *The Neocolonialism of the Global Village* with the University of Minnesota Press. Her forthcoming book, Savage Mind to *Savage Machine: Racial Science and Twentieth-Century Design* (also with the University of Minnesota Press), has been supported by the Social Science Research Council, the Graham Foundation of Art and Architecture, and the College Art Association.

JOSEPH GODLEWSKI

Joseph Godlewski is an Assistant Professor at the Syracuse University School of Architecture and the author of the theory anthology *Introduction to Architecture: Global Disciplinary Knowledge* (Cognella, 2019). He holds a Ph.D. in Architecture from UC Berkeley. His writing has been featured in various forums including *The Plan Journal, e-flux, Architecture Research Quarterly, CLOG, MONU,* ArchDaily.com, *Traditional Dwellings and Settlements Review,* and the book *The Dissertation: An Architecture Student's Handbook* (Routledge, 2014).

IVONNE SANTOYO-OROZCO

Ivonne Santoyo-Orozco is an Assistant Professor of Architecture at Bard College where she co-directs the emerging Architecture program. She holds a PhD in architecture from the Architectural Association and a Master degree from the Berlage Institute. Her research explores architecture as an interface between contemporary forms of governance and capital. She is currently at work on an architectural genealogy of property regimes in Mexico.

JAKE MATATYAOU

Jake Matatyaou is a Lecturer at UCLA Architecture and Urban Design and a founding partner of JuneJuly, a design consultancy based in Los Angeles, CA, and Seattle, WA. Using architecture as a visceral mode of communication, Matatyaou's research explores the impact of globalization and networked technology on the spaces, places, and people of contemporary cities. His work draws from interaction design, experience design, film, and music, to offer a renewed interest in the human body and its situation in the world.

GABRIEL FUENTES

Gabriel Fuentes is an Assistant Professor at Kean University's School of Public Architecture where he directs the Master of Architecture program. His research intersects architecture, culture, and politics, especially as these participate in world-making projects (i.e. heritage, modernities, revolutions, etc.). His writing has appeared in *Log, The Journal of Space Syntax, e-flux architecture, The Architect's Newspaper,* and *Future Anterior.* He is a winner of the 2020 ACSA/Buell Center Course Development Prize for "Unthinking Oil: Public Architecture and the Post- Carbon Imaginary.

ELISA DAINESE

Elisa Dainese is an Assistant Professor at Dalhousie University, School of Architecture. She works on issues of decolonization, global history, architectural design and urbanization with a focus on the transoceanic exchange between Africa, Europe, and America. She holds a PhD from the IUAV, in Italy. Her research has received grants and awards from Columbia University, Bruno Zevi Foundation, CCA, SSHRC, GAHTC, and the Graham Foundation. Her book projects include two manuscripts entitled *War Diaries: Design after the Destruction of Art and Architecture* (co-editor, University of Virginia Press, 2021) and *African Dimensions of Postwar Architecture: A Global History of the Sub-Saharan "Habitat"* (author forthcoming).

MATTHEW ALLEN

Matthew Allen is a lecturer at the University of Toronto who researches the history and theory of architecture, computation, and aesthetic subcultures as they pertain to pressing contemporary ecological and social issues. Allen is the author of *Architecture becomes Programming: Modernism and the Computer, 1960-1990* and essays in venues such as *Log, e-flux, Domus,* and the *Journal of the Society of Architectural Historians.* He holds a PhD and a Master of Architecture degree from Harvard University.

ANTONIO FURGIUELE

Antonio Furgiuele is an Associate Professor at Wentworth Institute of Technology, School of Architecture and Design. His research focuses on the histories and theories of information and communication technology. He has a master's degree in History, Theory & Criticism of Architecture from MIT. He was a Research Fellow at University of Wisconsin - Milwaukee and at the MacDowell Colony.

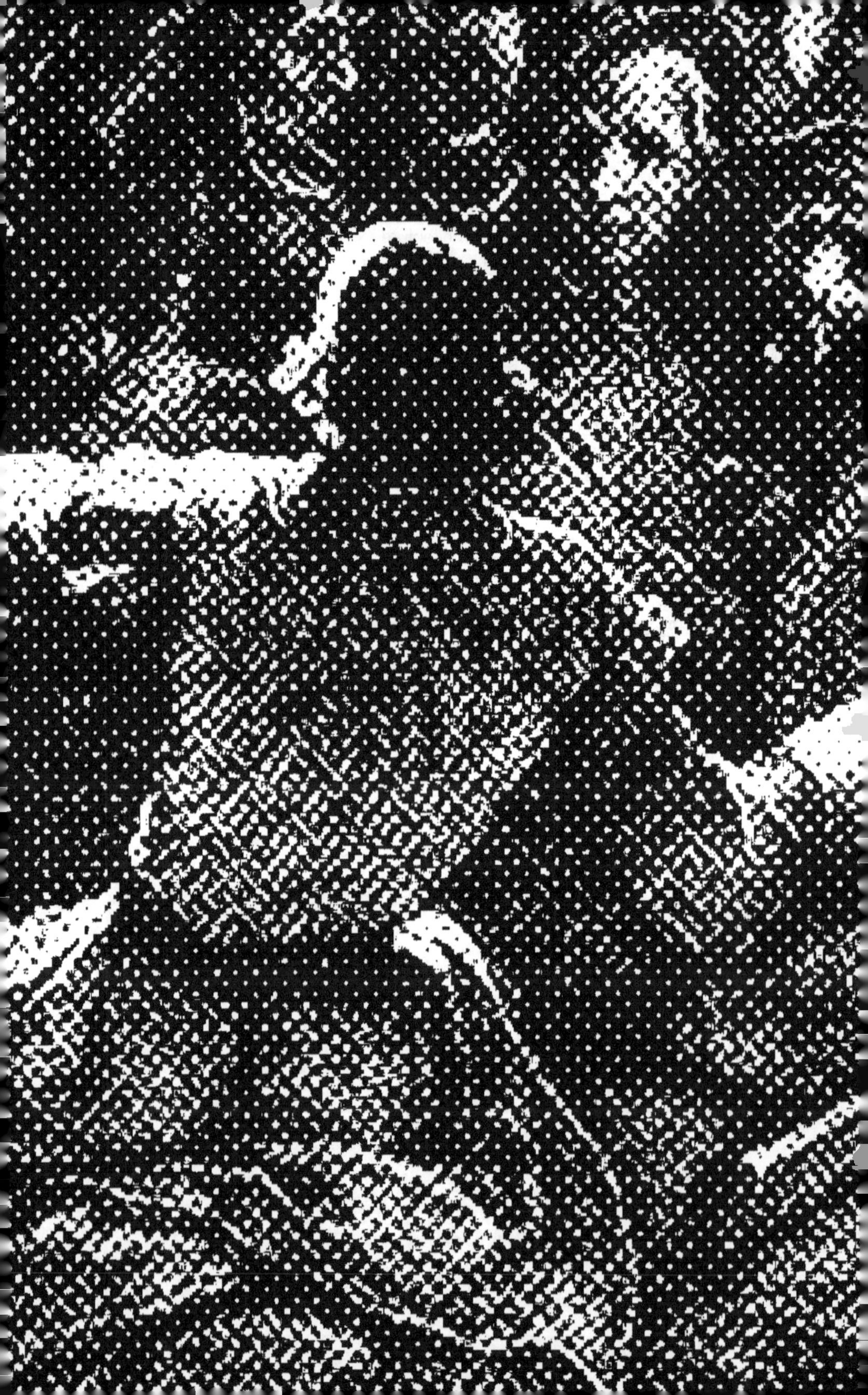

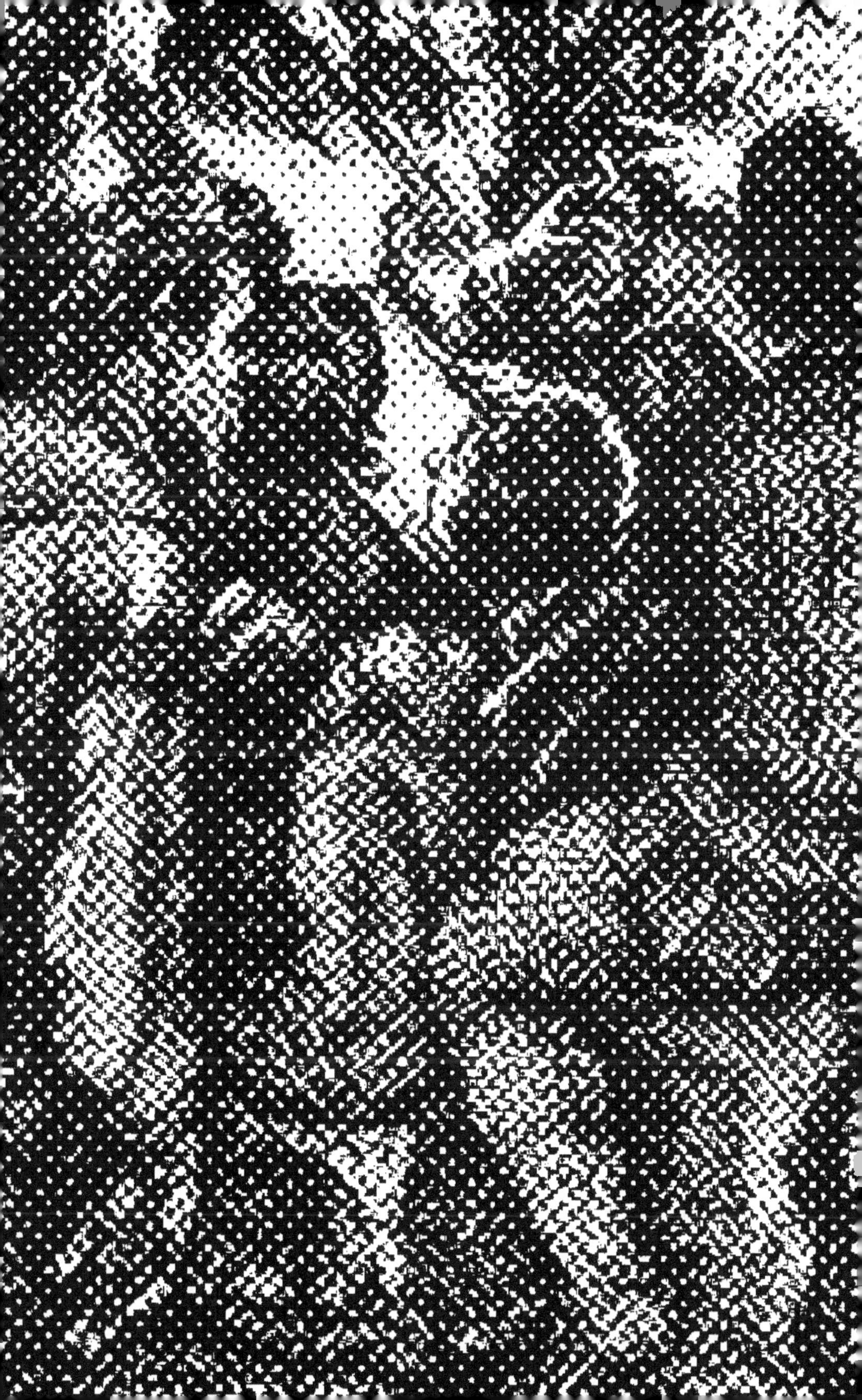

ÆP

Editor
Joseph Bedford

Copy & Content Editor
Corinna Anderson

Graphic Design
Twelve (www.twelve.la)

Layout Design
Sarah Schaffer (@schaffer.design)

Website
architecture.exchange

Instagram
@architectureexchange

Facebook
@thearchitectureexchange

Twitter
@_archexchange

Published by Architecture Exchange Press
Typeset in *MF Bespoke* by metaflop
Endpages by Cornelis van Haarlem, *Antrum Platonicum,*
1604, engraving." Source: British Museum.

ISBN: 978-0-9983750-2-1

www.ingramcontent.com/pod-product-compliance
Lightning Source LLC
LaVergne TN
LVHW010703110826
845149LV00014B/3212

* 9 7 8 0 9 9 8 3 7 5 0 2 1 *